A Mighty Fortress

A MIGHTY FORTRESS

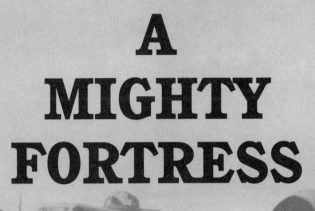

Lead Bomber Over Europe

CHARLES ALLING

Edited by Elizabeth Alling Hildt

CASEMATE
Havertown, Pennsylvania

Photo on pages xiv, 20, 26, 44, 50, 68, 76, 90, 106, 120, 138, 150, 160, and 172 courtesy of USAAF.

Published by
CASEMATE
2114 Darby Road, Havertown, PA 19083.

Typeset and design by K&P Publishing.

ISBN 1-932033-01-7

Cataloging-in-Publication data is available from the Library of Congress

First edition, first printing

PRINTED AND BOUND IN THE UNITED STATES OF AMERICA.

Contents

This work is dedicated to

Prudence "Prudy" Kelsey Alling
1923–1944

———— ◆ ————

and to

Ray Baskin and Bill Wright
and the other members of my crew:

> *Glen Banks*
> *Jack Brame*
> *Eddie Edwards*
> *Willie Green*
> *Mort Narva*
> *Chuck Williams*

Preface

This is a personal story. It's about what was. Every passage, every episode and every fact is true. It's about war—World War II, as seen through the eyes of one pilot of a B-17 Flying Fortress in the Eighth Air Force. Once I had flown overseas to our base in Mendlesham, England, I said goodbye to life as I knew it. Over the next eight months, I flew twenty-seven missions over Germany, France, and Czechoslovakia, with more than two hundred and twenty hours flying over enemy territory.

When I revisit those moments, I am reminded of how fortunate I am. I do not understand why we made it back alive when so many others should have and didn't. For those who flew in the Eighth Air Force, I suspect we all may have felt, at some point, that we were living on the edge, knowing that each flight could be the last. This unspoken understanding, this common bond, inspired deep, lasting friendships. This was my experience with my crew. We were bound together with undivided affection and devotion for each other.

This book is a recollection of only those combat missions, experiences, and thoughts that are deeply imbedded in my mind. Before each sortie, Intelligence officers would brief us on what to expect. And then at the start of each flight, our Flying Fortress would lift herself gracefully, carrying between two and three tons of bombs. We'd break through the clouds with the sunlight dancing and sparkling on her silver wings. Behind us and to either side, flying in tight formation, were hundreds of planes, a formidable and a majestic sight.

I couldn't help but feel overwhelmed with pride for my crew, the Eighth Air Force, and my country. That gave me the strength I needed to carry on. I often savored those brief, peaceful moments, lulled by the hum of our engines, as we flew east over the English Channel, heading for enemy territory. Then, at times, all hell would break loose. But with a leap of faith, hope, and prayer—and a lot of luck—we made it through, and beyond.

———————•◆••———————

Years passed before I had any desire to contact my crew. I have often wondered why. Now it seems so clear. After VE Day, when I returned to the States and left the service, I was anxious to break away from the past and begin a new life. I was focused on a new beginning, a new direction. My crew, all dear to my heart, must have wanted to do the same, and I am sure each one of us decided privately to look ahead and not back. Over half a century passed; still, I always had a hunch that eventually I would retrace my steps.

Fifty-four years after the war, for some inexplicable reason, I felt bound and determined to find my crew. I made calls all over the country. It was the first time I had initiated contact since we had all said goodbye after our return to the States in 1945. Of the nine of us, after an exhaustive search, I was unable to locate Mort Narva, my radar navigator; Eddie Edwards, my radio operator; and Chuck Williams, my left waist gunner. I soon learned that Glen Banks, my co-pilot; Willie Green, my crew chief; and Jack Brame, my right waist gunner had died. I could locate only two surviving members: Ray Baskin, my navigator, and Bill Wright, my bombardier. When I called them on the phone, there was a moment of silence on the other end. Ray couldn't believe it, after all those years, and neither could Bill. Bill broke the stunned silence on the line, "You mean you're still alive? That's utterly impossible!"

The three of us knew a reunion was long overdue. We decided to meet in a central location, choosing Savannah, Georgia. On November 25, 1999, we gathered at the Hampton Inn. Ray and Bill met just before I arrived. After long hugs, they sat down together and renewed their friendship. Minutes later, nervous with anticipation, I walked in the entrance of the inn, the doors spun around, the wind whisked in and carried me along with it. I asked the clerk at the desk the whereabouts of my friends, fearing that after so much time I would not recognize them, and I entered the lounge where they were waiting. I cannot begin to explain the warmth I felt at that moment, and the joy that we were together again.

Inset: *Reunion of the crew of the* Miss Prudy *in Savannah, Georgia, November 1999. Charles Alling could only find two of his crew (top) when he searched for them fifty-four years after the war. Left to Right: Bill Wright, Charles Alling, Ray Baskin.* (Top photo: USAAF)

That was the start of our five-day reunion. I knew that if it didn't happen then, it would never happen at all. I am also certain that if I had ever walked past Ray or Bill on the street, I would have thought they were perfect strangers.

The next morning, we left for one of Georgia's Golden Isles, twelve miles east of Savannah, accessible only by boat. This would be the first and only time we had ever talked about our shared experiences. At the house we threw over gear into our rooms and headed out for a walk on the beach. Our pace, if you can call it that, was slow and deliberate, not because we were checking our footing—though on other terrain that would be of some concern—but because we were deep in thought about our combat missions from September 1944 to April 1945.

The three of us were full of spirit and willing to capture and recall our war experiences. We had, after all, shared the same space in a cold, damp Nissen hut for nearly a year. It had taken a lot of energy to maintain our composure and strength living in those quarters but we had found creative ways to make the Nissen hut a comfortable place—surrounding ourselves with photographs of loved ones that we tucked away carefully in our footlockers.

Now here we were, walking together once again, but this time on a vast stretch of beach with no one in sight for miles. Seagulls flew over head, dropping shells onto the beach, reminding us of flak in the skies over Europe. The shells fell onto the hard sand, cracked and split open, spreading the gulls' next meal before them. As we followed the water's edge, I was lulled by the waves washing against the shore. Bottle-nosed dolphins played in the surf, gliding along the crests of waves and guiding us along the water's edge. The dolphins reminded me of our "Little Friends," the P-47 and P-51 fighters that had guided our bomb group to and from enemy territory, protecting us from the Luftwaffe.

When we would fly back to our air base in England after a bombing raid, it was usually Bill who had broken the silence. Over the next few days, as we walked the beach and explored the island, Bill now initiated many of the conversations that helped us recount our past. Stopping in his tracks he'd say, "Well, I want to tell you something and this is God's honest-to-goodness truth. Now listen!"

The command issued, we came to attention, but one time, he wanted to ask us something. "What was the time you were most scared? I mean, really scared—when you were certain that you were going to die?" He didn't pause to hear our answer; he knew it. On January 20, 1945, we had our first terrifying brush with death and had survived only by a miracle. That was the worst of countless other occasions when a burst of flak, a fighter's cannon, or a mid-air collision could have brought us unexpectedly to our doom. With each step, sinking deeply into the fine sand that curled around our toes, leaving only our footprints to wash away in the tide, we now told each other how it had been and dared to relive our many close calls.

◆━●━◆

After our reunion, I returned home determined to write our story. I climbed the folding ladder up to our third floor attic, where I crawled on my hands and knees in the dark, searching for musty cartons of war mementos. I found two boxes full of letters, photographs, and other memorabilia that had been stowed away years before, deliberately out of reach and out of mind.

I wasn't sure where or how to begin this project until I realized the process was similar to painting a picture. The greatest effort is taking the first step to raise the brush to the canvas. So I started, putting down in long-hand small passages and bits of memories for this book, fortunate to have guidance and inspiration along the way.

I extend my heartfelt gratitude to those who gave me their support and guidance:

Ray Baskin and Bill Wright. Thanks for your special insights, your lasting memories, and long friendship.

My daughter and editor, Beth Alling Hildt. You took over this manuscript after I had given it the best I had. This ever-loving, talented, and beautiful woman burned the midnight oil, unearthed my past, provided significant historical research, added pertinent poetry, molded the manuscript, and stepped up the pace.

My wife, Gail. You helped clear my thoughts and provided precision and imagination when needed, so I could unravel my recollections of a half century ago.

My assistant, Becky Welch. You were always there when

I called, always encouraging, and took the extra mile as you typed and never complained.

My good friend, Peter Huchthausen. Your article about Dresden ignited the spark that got me moving on this project. I thank you, also, for your counsel and good friendship.

My literary agent, Alex Hoyt. You've had great faith in me and I am indebted to you for seeing this process through.

My publisher, David Farnsworth. Your decision to take on this project is more important to me than you can imagine.

My cheerleaders, Monty Scharff, M. L. Norton, Gil Perkins, Junie O'Brien, and Clarke Oler. You were always willing to read my manuscripts, and your enthusiasm and encouragement were constant.

My son-in-law, Brad Hildt. I will always appreciate your humor, compassion, tireless devotion, and your insistence that I limit your acknowledgment to a single page.

Librarians, Carol Whitten and Merry Hermans at the Kennebunk Free Library, and Mary Prokop at the Mighty Eighth Air Force Heritage Museum in Savannah, Georgia. I will never forget your tenacious research.

Betty Atwood, Gerry Hotchkiss, Dave Richardson, Charlie and Clare Rimmer, Phil and Betsy McMaster, John Corse, Dave Binger, Jack and Joan Wuerth, and Barry Boardman. Your lively contributions to this process were invaluable.

And finally, my devoted, handsome, black labrador retriever, Archie. You nipped and tugged at my pant legs, sensing my recovery from a life threatening illness that nearly brought this project to an abrupt halt. Each nip, pull, and tug was an encouraging signal that it was time to move forward to see the completion of this book.

HIGH FLIGHT

Oh, I have slipped the surly bonds of earth
And danced the skies on laughter-silvered wings;
Sunward I've climbed, and joined the tumbling mirth
Of sun-split clouds—and done a hundred things
You have not dreamed of—wheeled and soared and swung
High in the sunlit silence. Hov'ring there,
I've chased the shouting wind along, and flung
My eager craft through footless halls of air.
Up, up the long, delirious, burning blue
I've topped the windswept heights with easy grace
Where never lark, or even Eagle flew.
And, while with silent, lifting mind I've trod
The high untrespassed sanctity of space,
Put out my hand, and touched the face of God.

—John Gillespie Magee Jr.

In December, 1941, Pilot Officer John Magee, a nineteen-year-old American who served with the Royal Canadian Air Force in England, was killed when his Spitfire had a mid-air collision. Several months before his death, he composed this sonnet, a copy of which he mailed to his parents in the United States.

Ten years after the war, I was seated next to his father, John Magee Sr., at a dinner in New York. I suspect he always carried this sonnet with him. That night he gave me a copy.

—Charles Alling

1

Through a Glass, Darkly

December 6, 1941   At 9:30 P.M., a Navy commander climbed the stairs to the second story of the White House, entered a large oval study, and gave President Franklin D. Roosevelt an intercepted and decoded cable from the Japanese government to its ambassador in Washington. The president pored over the rather lengthy cable for about ten minutes. He then handed it to Harry Hopkins, his chief foreign policy aide. Hopkins read with dismay what amounted to a Japanese rejection of all attempts to peacefully resolve the differences between the United States and Japan. He handed the cable back to the president. A moment passed. Then Roosevelt turned to Hopkins and said, "This means war." Hopkins nodded, adding that the Japanese would strike when they were ready and wherever they chose. It was unfortunate, he suggested to the president, that the United States could not strike first, since the alternative was to suffer surprise attacks on its own Pacific interests or on those of the European nations who were also embroiled against Germany.

"No," Roosevelt replied, "we can't do that. We are a democracy and a peaceful people." The United States could not strike first; it would have to wait for the blow which would subsequently turn the wars in Europe and Asia into a World War. Neither Roosevelt nor Hopkins realized, as they discussed the issue late into the night of December 6, 1941, that the Japanese Combined Fleet had already crept to within striking distance of America's primary naval base in the Pacific. Their wait would be over in only a few hours.[1]

December 7, 1941   It was a quiet Sunday afternoon at Wesleyan University, Middletown, Connecticut. My roommate, Bill Blelock, and I were reading in our room. At 2:30, a friend rushed in shouting the alarming news: the Japanese had attacked Pearl Harbor. We became glued to a small radio in our room, listening in disbelief to the news, searching for reports that provided answers to an endless stream of questions. That single event would change countless lives and transform both America and the world. Two days later, President Roosevelt addressed the nation and declared: "We are going to win the war." He also promised, "We are going to win the peace that follows."

The following morning, Bill and I walked into town from campus to enlist. Bill joined the Marines and I signed up for the Army Air Corps. I stood in a line with scores of young men eager to add their names to a list and eager to defend their country. There was never a shred of doubt that this was the right thing to do. America had been attacked. I returned to campus after signing papers for the Air Corps Aviation Cadet Program. A few days later, I received a letter from the Air Corps stating that with a backlog of applications, I would have a six to twelve month wait. That was fine with me as it would give me time to complete my sophomore year. But studies were often overshadowed by even greater attention paid to the U.S. build-up and its deployment of forces.

Two weeks later, over Christmas, I was home in Montclair, New Jersey, for vacation break, and I called on my good friend and neighbor, Gordy Gates. Gordy had enlisted earlier in the fall, and his number had come up fast. He told me that he was leaving Yale University to join the Air Corps. "This is the best branch of service, Charley. Let's go!" Perhaps because of the reports on the Battle of Britain, I was already taken with the idea of becoming a pilot, and his enthusiasm was all the more compelling.

Our friendship had begun in our early years, and by high school we had formed a strong bond. Often we'd meet up with each other on our way to and from school and went on double dates in high school, going to the movies and a local restaurant for a coke and gingerale—sometimes a beer or two. It was never difficult for Gordy to find a date; he was a handsome, dark-haired guy, well-liked and respected. We were both on the track team: he was a broad jumper and I ran the high hurdles. Gordy nominated me for captain, and by the end of the season, our team had won the state championship.

I had a chance to say goodbye to him just before he left for cadet training. "Gordy, I'm right there with you. I don't know where I'll be sent, but let's stay in touch and hopefully we'll find ourselves on the same continent. Be safe, guy," I said affectionately as I did only with my best friends, and we shook hands.

By February 1943, I received a call from the Air Corps. I had to drop my books and had only two weeks to report to duty at Atlantic City for indoctrination into the Air Corps. The weekend before I left college, we had our winter house party. My date, Alison Walker, came down to Connecticut from Boston. Alison, known affectionately by her friends and admirers as Sonny, was a lovely brunette whose portrait was once featured on the cover of Life Magazine, modeling a sailor's cap. Sonny was a lot of fun, and a wonderful dancer. During her visit we never talked about the war, and that made our time together all the more poignant. On Saturday night, we all danced the jitterbug, the lindy, and the foxtrot to the recorded music of Tommy Dorsey, Glenn Miller, and Count Basie. The rhythm and beat of the music were infectious as we danced on the brink of the unknown.

On Sunday afternoon, I put Sonny on the train back to Boston. Standing there alone I watched the train as it made its way from the station with dark smoke billowing from the stacks. As it disappeared into a thin line on the horizon, I turned and walked away, not sure when I would see Sonny again. This was the first goodbye of many as I was soon to leave for training for the war.

Three days later, I boarded a train from my home in New Jersey for Atlantic City. I was issued new attire: a brown, drab winter coat that hung inches off the ground, leather boots, several pairs of winter underwear, a woolen hat, and heavy gloves, and khakis. Young privates, like myself, were subject to harsh discipline. We learned to take orders—no questions asked. We marched in cadence up and down the boardwalk, hour after hour, doing about faces, right faces, left faces, starting before dawn in chilling temperatures. This experience would serve as an introduction to my life overseas, and prepare me for the bare bones operation I would come to know well.

There were times when we were summoned at 5:00 A.M. With a few minutes to dress, we'd race down the stairs, and step into formation. Sometimes we were left standing in the cold for half an hour and then ordered to climb back up the stairs to our rooms. An hour or two later, the procedure was repeated. We not only learned discipline, but we learned order and respect. The mental discipline, the mental toughness, would serve me well.

All of us endured psychological evaluations as well. During my first exam, I sat across the table from a psychiatrist, who seemed determined to leave me unsettled, and at one point he asked, "How old were you, Private Alling, when you last wet your bed?"

I thought an absurd question deserved an absurd answer. "Oh, probably around ten," and I shrugged my shoulders.

He stood up, looked at me sternly, put his pad down slowly and walked across the room, signaling to the other psychiatrists to join him. They assembled in a group and looked over at me quizzically. The huddle broke up, and the psychiatrists returned to the table, "Private Alling, that will be all!" That was the sign that I was a survivor, and for whatever reason, I had just earned my right to be trained as a pilot.

I next traveled by train to Maxwell Air Base in Montgomery, Alabama. This was the beginning of my training as a cadet. That's where I learned to eat a square meal while keeping a stiff posture, and to make a bed with the blanket so taut that if you dropped a dime on it, the dime would bounce back up. The harrassment from senior cadet officers was incessant. I wondered if I ever could have followed one of those officers into battle, but there was one exception, one guy who seemed to stand out from all the others. He walked over to me in the barracks and spoke in a commanding voice, "Cadet, sound off your serial number!" As I gave him my name, rank, and serial number, he gave me a nod and an understanding smile. I thought, "There's a good guy. I could follow him into battle."

Now ready for primary training, I left for Orangeburg, South Carolina, where I learned to fly a Stearman bi-plane. My instructor, Harlan, was assigned five cadets. We all loved this guy; he was like a father to us. We knew that some time between ten and fifteen flying hours, we would solo. This was the most important and memorable day for a cadet. At this point I knew I was meant to be a pilot. Some guys looked forward to being a navigator or bombardier, and a lot of them wanted to be gunners. I just wanted to fly the plane.

One day, Harlan took me to a grass airstrip a few miles from the

The author's cadet group: Charles Alling is on the far left; his instructor, Harlan is fourth from right; Cadet Wiggins is on the far right. (USAAF)

base to shoot landings. I thought, "Alling, pay attention! This is it!" As Harlan and I flew together over to the strip, he motioned from the open cockpit that it was time to land. The landing was fine. I taxied back to the take-off spot and repeated the process. I noticed my hand was sweaty and my forehead was sopping wet. I hoped this wasn't a telltale sign. But after the second landing, Harlan motioned for me to taxi off the strip. When I stopped, he jumped out and called to me above the rumble of the idling engine: "Take her around twice, cadet!"

I nodded and taxied off. This was it; there was no turning back. Reaching the strip, I stopped at the end and pushed the throttle forward a little to test the spark plugs. I gave her the gun and off we flew up to a thousand feet, making two ninety degree turns to the left to put me downwind and parallel to the strip. I flew a few miles from the field, made two more ninety degree turns to face the landing area upwind. As I approached the field, I gradually reduced the power and descended. As we passed the end of the runway, ten feet from the ground, I chopped the power and we settled in. It was only a fair landing, but as Harlan and other instructors would tell us, "Any landing you walk away from is a good one."

I repeated the landing practice and when I was flying downwind, I felt free, forgetting that I was going over a hundred miles per hour. I had to rein in my enthusiasm and remind myself, "Alling, not so cocky or you'll lose it!" I landed and taxied over to Harlan. He was standing there grinning, his hands on his hips, his flying helmet pushed back over his forehead, and his white silk scarf flapping freely in the breeze.

On a subsequent flight with Harlan, I did all the usual spins, and then he motioned to me to strap in. I gave him a thumbs up, and with that, he flipped the plane over and we flew upside down, held in only by the straps. I looked into the mirror and saw him smiling. He must have seen that I was smiling as well. I had fallen in love with flying; it was exhilarating. But I was not an acrobat, and I wasn't the kind of guy who wanted to fly upside down in a nimble fighter. I'd rather fly a four-engine bomber. I knew that once I got my wings, I hoped to fly a large aircraft, preferably a B-17 Flying Fortress.

Just days later, I had some time off, and enjoyed a relaxing day on the air base. I was feeling confident. Things were going well, better than I had ever anticipated. I was talking with a bunch of guys clustered around the planes when I received word from an officer that there was an important message for me in the office. My parents had sent me a telegram with news that Gordy Gates had died. He had been flying a P-47 Thunderbolt fighter against the Japanese in New Guinea, and had crashed.

Gordy's family was devastated. Needless to say, so was I. This was the first time that I had experienced the death of such a close friend, and in the years that followed, I often thought of Gordy. Tragically, he never had a chance to reach his potential; the country had lost a hero that it barely knew. But I and others had known him. Normally, the sudden death of a dear friend requires a certain closure. In wartime, however, that was something we were all denied.

Charles Alling after his first solo flight in a PT-17 on September 23, 1945. (USAAF)

A week later, I was sent to Sumter, South Carolina, for basic flight training. Something about that base seemed dead serious. We trained in a Vultee monoplane with a powerful engine and small wings. The instructor greeted us less than cheerfully: "This is a dangerous plane. Don't ever get into a spin because you'll never pull out."

On Thanksgiving Day, I was flying solo at five thousand feet. (The rule of thumb was that when you were practicing stalls and other stunts, you had to fly at a minimum of five thousand feet.) My plane fell into a spin and in a matter of seconds, I lost 4,500 of those feet. I pulled out at five hundred feet leaving myself a fraction of time before impact. I never felt dizzy. I just knew I had to stay cool, kick the rudder, dump the nose, and as she straightened out, pull back on the stick. When it was over, I was in a full sweat. "Holy s---!" I thought, "I can't let that happen again." It was a close call. Little did I know that worse was to come in Europe, and then with a full crew depending on my reactions.

That incident forced me to an alertness of how dangerous even training flights could be. I had to admit that being a cadet was a novelty, somewhat thrilling and even a bit glamorous, but now I realized the stakes were high. Our instructors were deliberate in their methods and they pushed us to our limits. Mistakes could be fatal. We flew in bad weather, we flew at night, and we flew at odd hours. We were trained to get ourselves out of a jam, no matter how it should happen or whatever it took.

One night at 8:00 P.M., we were driven to a small grass airstrip a few miles away. It was pitch black. We were assigned to fly a flight pattern with four ninety-degree turns to the left, then land and repeat the drill three times. The object of this exercise was to teach us to rely on instruments. We had to land on a grass landing strip where there were two barely discernible lights at the end of the strip. I made the usual turns and after a couple I took a quick look to be sure I could still see those lights. I was in a cold sweat, unable to locate the lights from any direction. I kept wondering, "What the hell will I do if I don't see those lights on the field?" Watching the instruments with great intensity, I finally landed the plane safely. After the wheels touched down, I gunned the motor, took off down the runway past the dim lights, and left for another go around. At the completion of these maneuvers, I taxied to the perimeter, cut the engine, and leapt out of the plane. I never talked about that experience—it was too frightening at the time. It was only later that I realized the instructors were preparing us for English fog, missions where even in broad daylight one couldn't see fifty yards on either side.

We had two more night visits to that grass airstrip. It wasn't much better the second and third time. In fact, it was worse. I felt as if I was holding onto life by a thread. I would have swapped ten combat missions for one of those nights; but after those flights, I no longer considered the airplane as my boss—it was my friend.

Finally prepared for advanced flight training, I left for Freeman Field in Seymour, Indiana. That's where I became great friends with a guy from Madison, New Jersey. His name was John Howe. John was the Cadet Corps commander, a leader of three hundred cadets. We went to classes together and flew in the same squadron. After hours, we talked in the mess hall and sometimes we'd grab a drink later in town. John loved being a cadet officer. He fit the role well and other cadets looked up to him. A tall, dark-haired guy with deep blue eyes, he walked with his shoulders back, and when he stepped into a room people would turn and take notice. He was commanding in a quiet way and he knew it.

During advanced training the die was cast. We took turns flying pilot and co-pilot with other cadets. Those who flew a twin-engine were headed to fly bombers. Those who went to the single-engine training base, would be flying fighter planes. I flew a twin-engine plane with a dual cockpit.

One night I flew a round trip—navigation training flight—to and from Indianapolis. It was a clear night. Confident in the other cadet pilot, I was flying co-pilot as he had done the same for me. I closed my eyes to rest for a few minutes, and then I sensed an unexplained sense of urgency. I glanced over at the instruments and looked at my pilot, only to find that he was dozing off, leaning on the wheel, pressing it forward and to the right. The plane was banking to the right and we were losing altitude rapidly. Both of us, exhausted, had been lulled by the dull roar of the engines. I gave him a swift kick in the shins. He woke up, startled, read his instruments and leveled off the plane. We stared at each other for a moment. Another minute and the plane might have been irretrievable. It was too easy to fall prey to exhaustion in flight. That was another close call, and I learned an important lesson about the importance of co-pilots.

In the days that followed, we looked forward to graduation and receiving our wings and gold second lieutenant bars. On that occasion, the Army Air Corps decreed that we were now officers and gentlemen. About ten days before graduation, a number of cadets at the field were sent out on a night cross-country trip. By the time the planes returned to base, there was no ceiling and no visibility. The base was "socked in." The officer in the control tower told them they couldn't land. The only way out was to circle the field until fuel was low and if the base hadn't cleared by then, climb to five thousand feet, head the plane south on automatic pilot and parachute. Seven planes followed the instructions, and fourteen cadets bailed out safely, landing in cornfields close by. Several did not, and one was John Howe.

John and his cadet co-pilot tried to land on an auxiliary grass landing strip. John was confident in his abilities, and I am certain he had every reason to feel that he could land safely. As he made his approach in the dark and pouring rain, he must have realized, when it was too late, that he wasn't going to make it. I am sure he tried pulling up, but without enough power, stalled out. Tragically, his plane plunged to the ground.

That morning, the operations officer sent for me. Knowing that John was a good friend of mine, he asked that I escort his body back to Madison, New Jersey, for the memorial service. I was told, in no uncertain terms, that I persuade his father, Judge Howe, not to open the casket. He would have been horrified to see a body charred and mangled.

John had been just eleven days from receiving his wings. He also had been engaged to Mary Reynolds from Waterville, Maine. She was lovely with a genuine smile. They were a handsome couple and I am sure they would have been married before he went overseas.

I stayed with the Howes before the service as did Mary. There were times we had to get out of the house, and take long walks together, for it was emotionally draining. The Howes understandably took John's death very hard, particularly as he was their only child.

The Episcopal church was full for the service. There were flowers everywhere. I fought off tears listening to the haunting sound of Taps as I folded the American flag with another soldier and handed it to John's mother. Her face was soft, straining to hold back her tears. Her eyes were misty and her hands shook. Her husband stood by her side, holding her upright with his eyes fixed on the flag that would accompany his son to his grave. At the end of the service, I walked down the aisle with the Howe family, followed by his fiancée. How terrible it was to have a friend die in the prime of his life, and how terrible to die such a violent death. It all seemed barbaric.

My family lived in Montclair, just a twenty-minute ride from Madison. I asked my parents not to come to the service, and I told them I'd get a ride home to visit them before returning to Freeman Field. I needed a good night's rest. I was greeted by my parents, my sister, Prudy, and Peter, my faithful Collie, who trailed at my heels.

The next morning, I had to return to Seymour, Indiana, but before I left home, Prudy and I sat alone on our porch. We had a few minutes to catch up. She told me how happy she was. She had taken a year off from college and was working at a local General Electric plant to earn money. She planned to return to Hood College in the fall as a journalism major, and she was looking forward to entering her sophomore year.

My roommate from Wesleyan was one of many who was smitten with Prudy. He had come to visit with our family for a few days during the 1942 Christmas holiday, just before I left for training. I remember that the two of them sat by the fire, exchanging lines of Shakespeare.

Prudy was an exuberant girl. She was intelligent, a great athlete, and full of spirit and enthusiasm. When she smiled, her face lit up. Compelling in a soft way, she projected warmth and empathy; there was nothing hard or harsh about her. She constantly reached out to others. She was a man's woman, and a woman's friend. I loved my sister and she loved her brother. We knew that we had an unusual friendship. We didn't have to explain anything. We just seemed to understand each other and know what the other was thinking. We shared the same sense of humor and an appreciation for the absurdities in life.

Prudy had something she wanted to tell me. "OK, Bubby. I'm not sure when I'll see you again. Will you stop by before you head overseas?"

"You know I will if I'm given permission, but I just don't know," I replied.

"If you are to fly overseas and I do not have a chance to see you again, I want to say goodbye now and give you something to hold onto. I want you to take this psalm and carry it with you always. When you feel worried, frightened or anxious, hold onto this, and remember that I always love you and that I'm always with you." She gave me a copy of the 23rd Psalm in her handwriting. I gratefully accepted it and placed it in my coat pocket.

It was time to go and I could not miss the flight. We were both misty-eyed and clutched each other in a tight hug. I said goodbye to Prudy and my parents, and left home. There were many days that followed when I read the psalm for strength and peace of mind:

> *The Lord is my shepherd;*
> *I shall not want.*
> *He maketh me to lie down in green pastures:*
> *he leadeth me beside the still waters.*
> *He restoreth my soul:*
> *he leadeth me in the paths of righteousness for his name's sake...*

After graduating from the cadets, I was sent to B-17 First Pilot's School at Chanute Field, Champaign-Urbana, Illinois, midway between Chicago and St. Louis. I'll never forget my first flight in a B-17. I felt so comfortable in this powerful Flying Fortress, with its long, wide wings, majestic tail, and its four powerful Curtis Wright engines. My instructors had prepared me well in those seat-of-the-pants trainers. Now that I was in the cockpit of the queen of the skies, I had confidence I could do the job.

After a month or so I had a weekend pass, and took a train to St. Louis for a visit with my mother's sister, Aunt Mac, and her husband, Wallie Smith. That Saturday night they took me to their country club for dinner. The clubhouse, with its grand entrance and white pillars, stood at the end of a long, winding drive. I walked outside in the dimly lit gardens. This was another world, quite different from the world to which I had grown accustomed. I looked at the galaxy of stars and listened to the band that played some of my favorite melodies—"I'll Be Seeing You," "In The Mood," and "Chattanooga Choo-Choo." I savored the moment.

Soon relocated to McDill Air Base in Tampa, Florida, I was assigned a crew. We were asked to assemble in the hangar. We were a mixed group from all over the country; a bunch of guys from very different backgrounds. I wondered how we could all possibly work together. Before long, though, I knew we would.

Glen Banks, my co-pilot, was from Mingo Junction, Ohio. Glen and I were the same age, twenty-two. A nice looking fellow, short and stocky, he had just graduated as a pilot from the Aviation Cadets. He was married, and while we were overseas his wife had their first child. Glen had hoped to fly fighters, but by the luck of the draw, and the increasing demand for bomber crews, he was assigned to be with us. This was not to his liking, but he accepted it pretty well, and I was glad. Glen was a darned good pilot and a loyal guy.

Raymond C. Baskin, my navigator, was from Mason, Tennessee. He was twenty years old, kind and empathetic, sharp, smart, and competent. Ray knew where we were every minute of every flight; at least I believed he did, and I would have staked my life on it—in fact, I did many times. He was a stickler for accuracy and fairness, as his navigator's log would attest. But Ray was more. He didn't have a loud, boisterous laugh but a dry sense of humor, and when he smiled you knew it was funny.

Ray was raised on a cotton farm in western Tennessee. His family was short of money, food, and clothes, and experienced shelter problems common to the area at that time, made worse by the Depression. Ray entered the Army Air Corps in February of 1943, two weeks after his nineteenth birthday. After completing basic training at Miami Beach, he was sent to Sioux Falls, South Dakota, for radio operator and gunnery school. He was in his twelfth week of a sixteen-week program when he applied for cadet training and was accepted. Ray ended up in Santa Ana, California, for classification and pre-flight training. A cadet could apply for training as a pilot, navigator, or bombardier, and Ray was accepted for navigator training. Ray said that graduating from cadet school was like crawling out from under a rock that had been on his back for over a year, and the first salute he received from a base MP made it worthwhile.

Willie E. Green, my crew chief, was from Tuscumb, Alabama. He was twenty-three years old and married. He could take a motor apart and put it back together, and he had an uncanny sense for understanding the complexities of airplane mechanics. Willie had another wonderful quality: he was very conscientious and cared deeply about our crew. I often felt like saying to him, "Okay, Dad, what do I do now?"

Howard W. Edwards, my radio operator, was from Pitcairn, Pennsylvania. He was twenty-three years old. Eddie could pick up signals, decipher codes and get through to any radio station without effort. He was cocky, but that was, surprisingly, a redeeming characteristic.

James A. Brame and Charles G. Williams were my waist gunners. Jack was from Topeka, Kansas, and Chuck was from Berkeley, California. Both were state troopers in Kansas and California respectively before joining the Air Corps. Both were married and Chuck had a son. Both were thoughtful guys and I suspected the rest of the crew thought so, too. When they put their arms on your shoulders, you knew that no one would ever lay a hand on you.

George Rumbaugh, my tail gunner, was from Westfield, New Jersey. George was a tall, swarthy looking twenty-four year old, somewhat boisterous and full of life.

Ward A. Yarborough, my ball turret gunner, was from Albuquerque, New Mexico. Ward was our "baby." He joined our crew at the tender age of eighteen. He looked so young, I was sure he could never have had his parents permission to go to war if he had needed it.

Mal, my bombardier, was from Akron, Ohio. Mal was twenty-three when he joined our crew. Unfortunately, he couldn't tolerate flying and he told me he wanted to get out. Together, we went to the operations officer who persuaded Mal to stay with us until we got to Europe. He reasoned that they needed bomber crews overseas, and he said that once we were there, Mal would be relieved of flying duties and our crew could pick up another bombardier. The officer reiterated that no crew could be sent overseas unless it was up to full complement. I promised Mal that I would see to it that we would talk to the chaplain at the air base, who would get Mal the help he needed and deserved.

We were soon given orders to find our assigned plane for training. Told to take my crew to the third plane in line, I led them onto the tarmac, and as we reached the B-17, we stopped dead in our tracks. The words "Memphis Belle" were painted on the nose of the fuselage, along with the Belle of Memphis herself, wearing a light blue, skin-tight bathing suit, with lovely flowing blond hair and a set of killer legs. Underneath those long, shapely legs were paintings of twenty-five small bombs indicating the number of missions she had flown.

The *Memphis Belle* was the first B-17 Flying Fortress to finish her tour of twenty-five missions with the Eighth Air Force. When the *Belle* returned to the U.S. from England, it flew to a number of cities on a War Savings Bond promotion trip. By that time, she had already made a place for herself in history. By the time we climbed on board, the *Belle* was a battered, war-torn plane that had seen better days. The instrument panels were scuffed up and there were patch marks on the outer hull where she had been penetrated by enemy bullets and flak. She seemed like a tired and noble workhorse sent out to pasture, but she would still serve us well.

We flew the *Belle* practically everyday for the next two and a half months in final training and preparation for combat overseas. We spent hours sharpening our skills. Glen and I practiced landings and take-offs in the day and night, simulating two and three-engine attempts. We took long navigation flights over water to allow Ray to practice his celestial navigation. We didn't know if we were going to be sent on the southern route across the Atlantic to Italy to join the Fifteenth Air Force, or on the northern Atlantic route to England to join the Eighth Air Force. Either way, the stars, moon, and sun would be our only beacons.

We flew practice bomb runs dropping sandbags on coral reefs and wrecks in the Gulf of Mexico. For gunnery practice, a single-engine training plane pulled a sleeve, a three-hundred-foot rope with a piece of white cloth, that trailed behind as a target for the gunners when we flew by.

Three weeks before we were sent overseas, business leaders in Cuba invited our squadron to Havana for a goodwill visit. We flew to Cuba in the *Memphis Belle*. Being a highly publicized plane, she caused a bit of a stir. During our first night in Havana, we were guests at an elaborate dinner where Cuban businessmen and our ambassador were in black tie. We were dressed in our starched khakis.

The next evening, we attended a dinner dance at the Havana Yacht Club where each officer escorted a young Cuban lady. The parents brought their daughters and, of course, took them home at the end of the evening. They, too, were dressed for the occasion and proceeded to sit in the balcony looking down on the dance floor with full view.

My date for the evening was Angela Minero, a dark-haired, dark-eyed beauty. I will never forget how she looked at me. Her eyes were like a pool of dark water and she never took them off me. Her warmth was intense and when we danced—very slowly—I felt my legs shake. She never gave a hint or indication that she noticed it. I pulled her a little closer to help steady myself.

When the music stopped, I suggested we walk outside for some fresh air. A short distance away we sighted the marina where a large number of yachts were secured, and I thought it would be nice to go take a look. She agreed and took my hand. Our casual stroll ended abruptly when a tall, military police sergeant stepped in front of us and announced, "You're off limits, Lieutenant! Return to the clubhouse."

That was a slap in the face from a man with a comfortable job in the U.S. Army based in glamorous Havana. Deflated, I looked at Angela, and I could see tears welling in her eyes. Slowly, she let go of my hand as we went through the glass door into the clubhouse. That was the last I saw of Angela Minero.

—•—•—

Ten days before we were sent overseas, I received a message to report to the squadron tactical officer immediately. (He served as a disciplinarian and administrator of our group.) These officers were barely tolerated by the airmen, and were considered the "chicken s___" of the Air Corps. I walked into the office and saluted him. He spoke to me sarcastically and announced that he had just received a telegram from the American Red Cross, which he proceeded to read. "We have been asked to inform you that Lieutenant Alling's sister, Prudence, is dying of spinal meningitis. Her family requests immedi-

Charles Alling and other Yankee crewmen in Havana on September 14, 1944. (USAAF)

ate emergency leave. Signed, American Red Cross Director, Montclair, New Jersey."

The officer looked up from the telegram, pushed his glasses down on his nose and glared at me. His stare was cold. "Permission denied," he said. "This is just a trick to get you home on leave. I've seen this ploy too many times."

I looked him directly in the eye, leaning forward with determination and conviction, "If you don't do everything in your power to get me on the next flight home, I'm going to the commandant immediately!" This officer was an insult to the Air Corps.

Arriving at the hospital in Montclair, I went straight to the waiting room outside the intensive care unit where I found my mother and father. They explained there was a slim chance that Prudy might live, providing emergency measures were taken. But if they did, there was a high probability that she would remain a vegetable the rest of her life. My parents asked me the question that plagued them: "What do you think?" I knew there was no choice.

I walked into Prudy's room where she lay still, barely breathing, and stared at this beautiful, twenty-one-year-old girl of whom I was so fond. She opened her eyes, and there seemed to be a glimmer of recognition. She reached out her hand, just as she had always done so naturally to me and so many others. I took it in mine and spoke to her softly, "I love you, Prudy." I kept holding her hand and looking into those forgiving eyes that were yielding to death.

When it seemed the time had come for her to leave us, I spoke to her quietly. "It's okay, Prudy. You can go." And although she could barely speak, she looked at us with infinite love and affection, as if she, too, knew it was time, and that was her way of saying, "Goodbye." She took one last soft breath, closed her eyes, and then lay motionless as her spirit left us. "Prudy, we love you," I whispered with tears rolling down my cheeks, and my words echoed and faded down the long empty hospital corridor.

A nurse took Prudy's wrist in her hand to check her pulse, and then placed her hands over her chest. She looked at us with deep remorse, said, "I'm so sorry," and quietly left the room. Minutes later, after I lost track of the time, the nurse returned, took the sheet at the bottom of Prudy's bed and covered Prudy's sweet, forgiving face.

Prudy had been playing tennis five days before and had come home early complaining of a severe headache. The next day she was taken to the hospital. Tragically, penicillin was not on the market. Just a few months later, it was made available to all.

The memorial service was in our house. My father read Corinthians 13. The last two stanzas said everything about Prudy:

For now we see through a glass, darkly;
but then face to face: now I know in part;
but then shall I know even as also I am known.

And now abideth faith, hope, charity, these three;
but the greatest of these is charity.

I read the 23rd Psalm, not from The Book of Common Prayer, but from the handwritten passage that Prudy had given me on the porch the day after John Howe's funeral service. The paper was crinkled and slightly worn as I had carried it with me since I had last seen Prudy. My hands shook and my voice quivered as I read the words that had been dear to Prudy. After it was over, I said goodbye to the handful of close family friends and neighbors. Prudy's friends left, pained. My parents were distressed. On the heels of Prudy's death, their only son was heading off to war. Another loss would be unbearable for them.

Hours after the service, I was on my way back to Florida. Boarding an American Airlines DC-4 en route from New York to Tampa, I felt weighed down with sorrow. As I looked at the land passing underneath, I thought how different it would be in a few weeks when we would be flying over Germany.

When I stepped off the plane, my crew was there to meet me. Glen approached me, "Chuck, when we get our new plane, we'd like to name her 'Miss Prudy'."

I was overwhelmed. "Thanks guys. I can't tell you how much this means to me. I'm sure Miss Prudy will see us safely through." I put my arm around Glen, and with a nod to my crew, we walked together off the tarmac. It was a pilot's prerogative to name his ship, and most pilots named their Flying Fortress after their girl. This was different.

It was time to move on, and I could never look back. In very little time, I had lost my two closest friends and my sister, but I couldn't dwell on the sorrow that tugged at my heart. If I did, I'd crumble, and I couldn't let my crew down.

ONE SHIP DRIVES EAST

One ship drives east and another west,
While the selfsame breezes blow;
'Tis the set of the sail and not the gate
That bids them where to go

Like the winds of the air are the ways of fate,
As we journey along through life;
'Tis the set of the soul that decides the goal,
And not the storm or the strife.

—Ella Wheeler Wilcox[2]

2

Sun in the East, Dead Ahead

———◆———

September 1944　We received orders to depart for Europe. We were to fly from Hunter Field in Savannah, Georgia, to Valley, Wales, where we would be assigned to an Eighth Air Force base in England. Our flight would take us along the eastern seaboard up to Goose Bay, Labrador, then over Greenland to Iceland, and finally Wales.

One night before our departure, I had dinner with a friend and fellow pilot, Bart Bartholomay, and his wife, Fran. Both seemed a bit mischievous, and I knew they were up to no good. With a glint in her eye, Fran said, "We've decided that you need a mascot to take with you. We found him in the animal shelter." She produced a cute and obviously affectionate little canine. I could only wonder how the heck we were going to get a dog in our plane and fly him to England? How would we keep him warm, bathed, fed, and safe? But the black and white spotted terrier endeared himself with my crew, and we had to take him with us.

"What do you think, guys?" I asked. "Can we get him safely to England?"

"Don't you worry about it," they said. "We'll take good care of him."

My crew found a box which they filled with dirt. Our terrier, appropriately named Flak Happy, slept on the wooden floor in the waist of the plane, covered with a small woolen blanket. At each base, two devoted guys took turns spending the night with him in the plane.

On September 18, we left Hunter Field and flew directly north.

On the way we flew over the home of my aunt and uncle's farm on the eastern shore of Chestertown, Maryland. Our flight plan was visual, and we set out on our own course. At 10:00 in the morning we approached their home. I knew it well because my sisters and I had vacationed on their farm every summer and on many holidays. Jinny and Charley Kingsley were standing out on the lawn waving to us. I asked my bombardier to open the bomb bay door and drop a package. I tucked a note inside of a shirt and tied an apple to the shirt to serve as ballast. A few days later, a farmer who lived a mile or so down the road found the package in his field. He brought it to my uncle and reported, "I'm not very impressed with your nephew's bombing accuracy!"

Just after we buzzed Chestertown, Charley Kingsley phoned my parents to say I was on my way up the coast. Ray plotted our course to Montclair. As we passed over my home, it seemed as though the whole town was outside to say farewell. They had spread sheets out on the lawn that spelled my initials.

Before we started our second pass over my house, I asked my co-pilot Glen if he would fly so I could get a closer look. We weren't more than two hundred and fifty feet off the ground and I could see my mother and father in the crowd. I can only imagine the view from their perspective. The silver wings of our B-17 shimmered in the bright sunlight. She was a mighty twenty-ton fortress, seventy-four feet in length with a wing span of one hundred and three feet and a tail over nineteen feet tall.

We dipped our wings and then, with a burst of power, we flew toward the morning sun. "I guess we really shook up those folks," said Glen. He was making every effort to stay relaxed even though he was uncomfortable flying over a residential area.

I looked out the window and focused on my father. He was a soft-spoken gentleman who commanded respect, and was the most honest and ethical man I ever knew. He had graduated from Yale University at the age of nineteen and Harvard Law School at twenty-two, and started work as a lawyer shortly thereafter. My father always carved time out of his day for me. He always attended every important school event. I remembered him standing alone on the sideline of the football field, in his gray coat, a shade long, and his gray fedora hat. He was there to watch our practice. And today there he was, once again, to show support in another chapter of my life.

I kept him in sight as long as I could as we flew away—the image of my father shrinking rapidly. He was barely five-foot-four, and getting smaller by the moment, but I knew he stood tall. I took one last look as we continued our climb, and then we followed the sun in the east, dead ahead.

———•◦•—◉—•◦•———

After a night at Grenier Field, New Hampshire, we left for Goose Bay, Labrador, a six-hour, 900-mile trip. We flew over Presque Isle, Maine, and the Province of Quebec. We spent the night in Labrador where the brisk air made for sound sleeping. I knew it would be a long time before I slept between cotton sheets again.

At the dawn of the new day, the sun shone brightly. Ray took a fix on the sun and then the moon, the only navigational aids he would have until we reached Iceland where we could pick up radio signals. We estimated that this 1,550-mile leg of the trip would take us seven hours with a strong tailwind. Our cruising speed was 150 miles per hour. Our plan routed us over the southern tip of Greenland, 750 miles from Labrador. Ray's navigation was on target, and exactly when expected we saw Greenland off our left wing. The land was desolate and the icebergs were beautiful, though forbidding.

Once Greenland was beyond us, I noticed that ice had started to accumulate on the leading edge of our wings. This was a pilot's nightmare: ice disrupts the airfoil, reducing lift capacity and causing the plane to stall out. There was only one solution for breaking up the ice—we had to dive the plane straight down so that the increased speed and pressure would force the ice to flake off. Everyone put on their oxygen masks and we climbed up to twenty thousand feet. I called the crew to strap in tightly and hold on. I pushed the steering wheel forward, and we dove down at 250 miles per hour, generating as much G-force as the plane could stand. Our B-17 shuttered, rattled, and shook; it seemed that at any moment, she would burst open at the seams. We were taking a risk descending at this speed, because a wing could tear off from the sheer force of gravity. But once we leveled off at four thousand feet, the ice was gone. Flak Happy was given oxygen during our descent from twenty thousand feet, and was reportedly not pleased with the maneuver.

A half hour later, the controls started to feel less responsive. I glanced at the air speed indicator, saw the needle slowly descend, and knew ice was starting to form again. By chance, Eddie had just picked up a radio message from an A-20, a twin-engined attack bomber that was flying the same route over the ocean at nearly the same latitude and longitude. They reported warmer temperatures were found at five hundred feet where the ice would naturally break off our wings. We descended to five hundred feet and continued at that altitude for the rest of our journey to Iceland.

During this trip overseas, my bombardier, Mal, had a tough time. I knew he did not have a temperament for flying, but I didn't realize he was in such bad shape. Agitated beyond reason, Mal repeatedly threatened to jump out of the escape hatch. Ray and Glen had to hold him down, and at one point Ray had to sit on top of him to keep him still.

Once we landed at Reykjavik, we joined the crew of the A-20. All of us were relieved to have made it there safely. After a short overnight, we left for the last leg of our trip. After fifteen hours of flying over the gray North Atlantic, Ray charted us within a few miles of our destination in Valley, Wales. After landing we cut the engines and jumped out of the plane. We were thrilled to have land-ed on British soil, having flown 4,315 miles.

Flak Happy was given a rub down and an extra bone for being such a courageous member of the crew. Jack grabbed him and tucked him into his big trench coat. But when the military police drove up in a jeep, they spotted Flak Happy's nose peering out from under Jack's coat. The British did not allow pets brought into the country, and we were informed that Flak Happy would have to be quaran-tined for six months. "You can come and claim your dog then," they stated firmly.

We had a tough time saying goodbye to that little fellow. We never did see Flak Happy again and I never knew what happened to him. Flak Happy was our first casualty. It was now time for us to focus on our job, and soon we forgot about the little dog who I trust made his way to a warm home in the English countryside.

We took a train to London, and from there were driven seventy-five miles northeast to the air base of the 34th Bomb Group in Mendlesham, located on the northeast coast of East Anglia, a few miles from the English Channel and less than one hundred from the continent. Shortly after our arrival, I went to the chaplain to discuss Mal's future. Mal had flatly refused to ever fly again. The chaplain made arrangements for Mal to be relieved of his duties and transferred to a hospital.

I accompanied Mal on the way. We sat on the bench in the back of an army truck as pouring rain beat on the canvas roof during the two-hour trip through the English countryside. I had to leave Mal at the hospital; there was nowhere else for him to go and he was desperate for help. I was torn inside, wondering how he would fare. I had to leave my bombardier with a broken heart and broken mind. He'd have to learn to fend for himself in a ward with helpless men.

"Mal," I spoke to him softly, "stay well and get back to Mendlesham as fast as possible. I'll see you there. You can get a ground job at the air base. I'm going to be looking for you, Mal. Take good care, okay?"

Mal never responded. I gave him a hug goodbye and walked out of the hospital. That's how I remember Mal, sitting alone, motionless, his eyes protruding from their sockets like black stones. The other troubled men in the ward sat in their nightshirts, their bony legs dangling over the sides of their beds.

PRAYER FOR COURAGE

Why should I long for what I know
Can never be revealed to me?
I only pray that I may grow
As sure and bravely as a tree.

I do not ask why tireless grief
Remains, or why all beauty flies;
I only crave the blind relief
Of branches groping toward the skies.

Let me bring every seed to fruit,
Sharing, whatever comes to pass,
The strong persistence of the root,
The patient courage of the grass.

Heartened by every source of mirth,
I shall not mind the wounds and scars,
Feeling the solid strength of earth,
The bright conviction of the stars.

—Louis Untermeyer[3]

3

Heartbeat F Fox

◆

The final leg of our journey from London to Mendlesham was one of the few occasions when I took time to appreciate the beauty of the English countryside. We traveled through small villages, rural hamlets, past farms and cottages surrounded by a patchwork of fields, pastures, and hedge groves. It was a bucolic setting. None of us talked. We absorbed everything around us.

The Mendlesham air base seemed quiet but tense at that moment as the 34th Bomb Group was on its way back from a mission over Germany. A group of senior officers had gathered on the second floor deck of the control tower where they were "sweating it out," facing east and standing wordlessly, some scanning the horizon through their binoculars. They were waiting to count the B-17s as they returned. The officers knew exactly how long the mission should take and they checked their watches for the return of the planes, but the sky was clear and all was quiet.

Within minutes, we heard the faint hum, and then the growing roar of engines in the sky as tiny specks in the distance grew into a long line of B-17s. As the lead plane approached the airfield, I instinctively started counting planes, though I never knew how many were expected back. It seemed that some of them would not return and there would be empty hardstands and empty cots.

The tight formation that had taken off that morning was now returning a scattered line of planes. My heart was beating with anticipation. No one spoke as the stream of B-17s approached the airfield. Some of the planes shot off red flares signaling they had wounded on board and these were given first priority to land. Ambulances and fire trucks were on alert. Many of the bombers

Aerial view of Mendlesham airfield—home of the 34th Bomb Group during World War II. It was from this base that Charles Alling and the crew of Miss Prudy *flew their bombing missions.* (USAAF)

looked torn and battered by flak and a few engines had been knocked out, their props feathered. It was a vivid, and some might say frightening, introduction to the 34th Bomb Group. But I still thought that the returning ships—scars and all—appeared as a mighty armada.

* * *

Captain Brophy, the 7th Squadron operations officer, requested our presence at the briefing block where we would find our lockers and flying gear. "Someone there will direct you to your plane," he said. "Familiarize yourself and walk around. Tomorrow you will start ground school and your training." The orders were dead serious. It was time to earn our paychecks or ship out.

Life at the air base was quite simple, marked by a sense of order and mutual respect. We spent a few weeks in ground training, then formation flying and getting accustomed to our assigned plane. We were ready to rise at 4:30 or 5:30 in the morning, and when we did, we would quietly and expeditiously don our gear. From the moment we opened our eyes, no one spoke. In the early hours of the morning, silence was preferable; in fact, breaking the silence was unacceptable. In time, we slipped into a routine. After each mission, we were debriefed by intelligence, then we'd change and head over to the Officers' Club. If the 34th Bomb Group returned with-

out injury or loss, the airmen could be lighthearted, though generally speaking we were pensive.

This was the fall of 1944. By the previous spring more than 130
military airfields had sprung up in the English countryside, crowded
into an area northeast of London about the size of the state of
Vermont. Forty-two of these bases were designated for the Eighth
Air Force B-17 and B-24 four-engine bomber groups, and fourteen
were bases for the P-47 Thunderbolt and P-51 Mustang fighters that
we referred to as our "Little Friends." Always after we crossed the
English Channel, P-51s and P-47s flew with us to the target, protecting us from the German fighters.[4]

The Eighth Air Force consisted of three air divisions: the 1st
Division had thirteen B-17 bomb groups; the 2nd had fourteen B-24
bomb groups; and the 3rd had fifteen B-17 bomb groups. The 34th
Bomb Group was in the 3rd Division, having converted to B-17s
after flying B-24 Liberators on sixty-three missions during the spring
and summer. By our arrival in September, the 34th Bomb Group had
fully converted to Flying Fortresses. The 34th included four
squadrons: the 4th, 7th, 18th, and 391st. The 4th Squadron consisted of only the lead crews. The 7th, 18th, and 391st Squadrons were
operational. We were assigned to the 7th.

The size of the entire Eighth Air Force was stunning. When each
group was operating at full capacity, there was a total of 1,600
bombers and 1,200 fighters available for combat. Between airmen,
ground crews and other support personnel, the "Mighty Eighth"
consisted of 300,000 men.

*A P-51 giving protection to bombers on a mission across the English Channel.
These small planes along with the P-47s were referred to by the pilots of the B-17s
as our "Little Friends."* (USAAF)

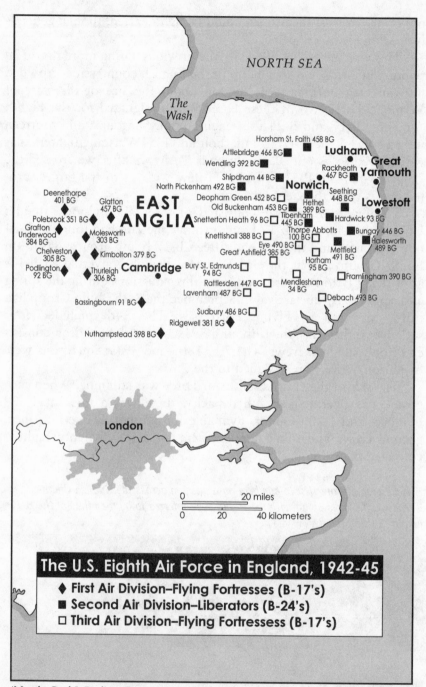

NORTH SEA

The Wash

Horsham St. Faith 458 BG

Ludham

Attlebridge 466 BG

Great Yarmouth

Wendling 392 BG

Rackheath 467 BG

Shipdham 44 BG

North Pickenham 492 BG

Norwich

Seething 448 BG

Lowestoft

Deenethorpe 401 BG

Glatton 457 BG

EAST ANGLIA

Deopham Green 452 BG

Old Buckenham 453 BG

Hethel 389 BG

Polebrook 351 BG

Snetterton Heath 96 BG

Tibenham 445 BG

Hardwick 93 BG

Grafton Underwood 384 BG

Molesworth 303 BG

Knettishall 388 BG

Thorpe Abbotts 100 BG

Bungay 446 BG

Chelveston 305 BG

Kimbolton 379 BG

Eye 490 BG

Metfield 491 BG

Halesworth 489 BG

Podlington 92 BG

Thurleigh 306 BG

Cambridge

Great Ashfield 385 BG

Horham 95 BG

Bury St. Edmunds 94 BG

Mendlesham 34 BG

Framlingham 390 BG

Bassingbourn 91 BG

Rattlesden 447 BG

Lavenham 487 BG

Debach 493 BG

Sudbury 486 BG

Ridgewell 381 BG

Nuthampstead 398 BG

London

0   20 miles

0   20   40 kilometers

The U.S. Eighth Air Force in England, 1942-45

♦ **First Air Division–Flying Fortresses (B-17's)**
■ **Second Air Division–Liberators (B-24's)**
□ **Third Air Division–Flying Fortressess (B-17's)**

(Map by Paul J. Pugliese. From *A Wing and A Prayer* by Henry H. Crosby. Harper Collins Publishers, 1993.)

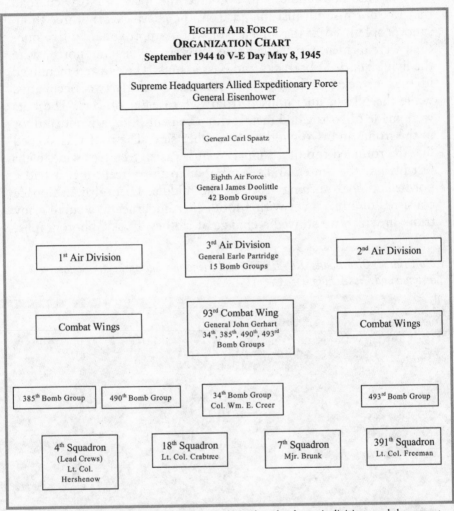

EIGHTH AIR FORCE
ORGANIZATION CHART
September 1944 to V-E Day May 8, 1945

Supreme Headquarters Allied Expeditionary Force
General Eisenhower

General Carl Spaatz

Eighth Air Force
General James Doolittle
42 Bomb Groups

1st Air Division

3rd Air Division
General Earle Partridge
15 Bomb Groups

2nd Air Division

Combat Wings

93rd Combat Wing
General John Gerhart
34th, 385th, 490th, 493rd
Bomb Groups

Combat Wings

385th Bomb Group

490th Bomb Group

34th Bomb Group
Col. Wm. E. Creer

493rd Bomb Group

4th Squadron
(Lead Crews)
Lt. Col.
Hershenow

18th Squadron
Lt. Col. Crabtree

7th Squadron
Mjr. Brunk

391th Squadron
Lt. Col. Freeman

The Eighth Air Force Fighter Groups were assigned to the three air divisions and they escorted the group within that division.

(Chart by Charles Alling)

The base at Mendlesham bordered the Ipswich-Norwich road that ran north-south just inland from the coast. Nearly three thousand people lived at the air base of whom approximately five hundred were airmen. On the left side of the road, heading north, were the living quarters: barracks and Nissen huts. The enlisted men lived in the barracks, each with a maximum of thirty-two occupants, while the Nissen huts housed from five to eight officers. The huts were made of corrugated metal with a cement floor, a wooden door in the front, and two windows on either side. The roof was shaped like the rounded top of a tunnel. A hut was sixteen feet wide, eight feet high at the center, and twenty-four to thirty feet long. It had a pot-bellied coal burning stove in the middle. Each airman's space consisted of a metal cot with a footlocker underneath; a small army trunk in which we stowed a change of clothes, books, photographs,

Mort Narva, Glen Banks, Ray Baskin, and friend in front of the 4th Squadron insignia and Nissen huts. (USAAF)

letters, writing paper, rosaries for some and other cherished mementos. Our conventional uniform—olive drab woolen shirt and pants—was carefully placed on metal hangers above our cots. The nearby ablution hut, always damp and cold, served the daily bathing needs, with the exception of showers that were accessible once a week in a hut half a mile away.

The squadron's operations office was located in the center of the compound and was shared by the commanding major or lieutenant colonel and an operations officer. There, notices were tacked and orders handed out. It was where you went to get your problems solved, your "ticket punched," as we were warned, and where disciplinary action was meted out.

On the opposite side of the road, there was a hangar where aircraft were repaired, and three macadam runways. The two short runways crossed the long runway that ran six thousand feet east-west into the prevailing wind, bordered by three and a half miles of perimeter track. Nearby there were a host of offices and buildings for operations and maintenance: a group commander's office with operating staff, the briefing block, ordinance depots, motor pool, coal yards, broadcasting station, fire house, machine shops, gas tanks, armament, engineering and maintenance depots, and a pistol range. The bomb site storage held thousands of bombs (250-, 500-, 1,000-, and 2,000-pound bombs) and was a considerable distance from operations, fenced in and carefully guarded.

Within days of our arrival, we were scheduled for our first mission. After a year and a half of training, we were ready for enemy action. Our morale was high. We almost felt like combat veterans, although we didn't have a clue what was in store for us.

Our first mission would take us to Metz in northeastern France, where General George Patton's Third Army was engaged in a fierce battle with the German Wehrmacht. We were assigned to fly tailend Charlie, the last plane in the low squadron. After the briefing, we were delivered to our Flying Fortress. Every B-17 was lovingly cared for by ground crews, as described by the 34th Bomb Group Association:

> Many mechanics worked into the night to prepare the bombers for duty—controls and instruments were tested, the landing equipment was inspected, the armament was checked

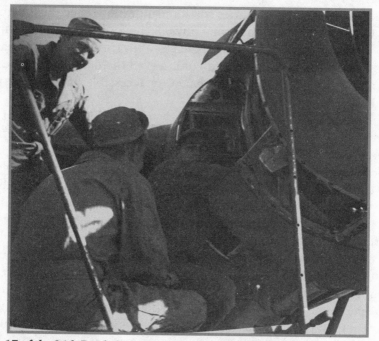

A B-17 of the 34th Bomb Group is prepared for a flight by the ground crew (above) and below a plane is loaded with the bombs to be dropped on the mission.
(Top photo: USAAF / Bottom photo: courtesy of Squadron/Signal Publications)

and, most importantly, the engines were checked for any signs of trouble. In the early hours of the day of the mission, often before sunrise, the planes were loaded with the delicate balance of fuel and ammunition. The distance to the target, anticipated wind speed and the projected cruising altitude were all taken into account to make the balance. The B-17 required 2,800 gallons of fuel for a mission into Germany. The B-17 burned 400 gallons an hour on its ascent to cruising altitude and 200 gallons while en route to the target. The allocation of gasoline normally didn't allow for a payload of bombs to be carried on the return trip, and if a mission was aborted the airmen were often faced with the task of dropping the bombs on targets of opportunity to ensure there was enough fuel to arrive back in England.[5]

Once we were delivered to our Flying Fortress, Glen and I walked around the plane checking for possible objects such as wrenches or cables that could have been left in or around the exterior after a night's work by the ground crew. We then tossed our gear up into the escape hatch in back of the pilot's seat, grabbed onto either side, and pulled ourselves into the plane, feet first.

For this mission, we were assigned a bombardier from the "pool" to replace Mal. He checked each bomb to be sure that the fins and fuses were in place. Once we joined the bomber stream and settled down for our trip, he'd set the bombs. Ray reviewed the charts, Eddie checked his radio, including the high and regular frequency channels, and the gunners went through their checklist. Crew chief Willie Green watched over everything. I knew he held the responsibility for making sure that this Flying Fortress was running smoothly. It was reassuring to have him seated just behind Glen and me.

I settled in. This flight was estimated for five and a half hours, unlike the average mission that lasted eight hours. Glen took the checklist and began, "Controls." I checked for freedom of movement of ailerons, rudders, and elevators. We lowered and raised the flaps to make sure they worked correctly. We uncaged the gyrocompass, an instrument that registers the rate of climb. Then we ran up each of the four Wright Cyclone engines, and in turn, feathered and unfeathered the props of each one. Planes now began to leave the

Above: *The instrument panel of the B-17 Flying Fortress.* (Courtesy of the Squadron/Signal Publications)
Inset: *B-17s of the 34th Bomb Group on a mission over Europe.* (USAAF)

hardstands and creep along. We were the last in take-off position. By now, the lead and deputy were flying above the clouds waiting for their flock to join them.

We were assigned to fly *Gotta Haver*, and for this mission its code name was *Heartbeat F Fox*. We were to follow *Heartbeat S Sam*. Glen made the crew check. I noticed that for once all our voices sounded tentative, somewhat hesitant, including Glen's when he said, "Sam's moving."

"Brakes off," I said, and we were on our way.

I gave a thumbs up to Bruce Sothern, our ground crew chief. I knew Bruce and his crew had been working on their "baby" in the early hours of the morning, making sure everything passed their instrument checks. Bruce turned to face *Gotta Haver*, took off his cap and saluted.

I taxied slowly, following a line of planes ahead. Concentration was at its peak. "Flaps down one-third," I said. I taxied to the very end of the runway to take advantage of every foot of macadam. When it was our turn, I inched over and turned the plane to face west upwind and stopped. I inched the throttles forward, and when the plane started to quiver and shake, I released the brakes. She moved slowly at first, then gathered momentum and headed down the runway. My left hand was locked onto the steering wheel and my right hand gripped the throttles.

Sam's wheels had just left the end of the runway ahead. I edged the throttles forward to full power and we sped ahead with conviction. I honestly felt confident and in charge. These bombers were large, heavy, complicated aircraft, but the Fortress also had a certain grace. I knew that when she was ready to fly, she would lift herself off the tail end of the runway, carrying 2,780 gallons of fuel and two and a half tons of bombs.

As we moved down the runway, Glen called out the air speed. We knew we had little time to reach the required speed to enable this heavy machine to reach a gradual lift off, otherwise we would need to immediately hit the brakes and pull over to avoid a stream of B-17s coming up from behind. But, at this moment she wanted to fly. I eased back on the wheel ever so slowly and she responded. "Wheels up!" I called, and it was reassuring when I heard a thud knowing the wheels were in and now there would be less drag.

"Navigator to pilot," called Ray, "your heading is 170 degrees."

"Roger 170," I responded.

I could not see anything through the clouds, and I watched the instruments carefully, keeping an eye on the manifold pressure. (The manifold pressure gauge indicates the amount of power you pour into the engine, and our take-off power was set at forty-three inches of manifold pressure.) As we climbed, I eased the engines back to thirty-eight inches—the climbing pressure. Our speed was one hundred and fifty miles per hour, and I kept it there. Glen, Willie, and I never took our eyes off the instrument panel.

At the briefing, we had been told to expect to break through the clouds at five thousand feet. The officers were on target. I could almost feel the sighs of relief from each man in the crew, some of

Colonel William E Creer, commanding officer of the 34th Bomb Group. (USAAF)

them nearly breathing down my neck. "That should be our group at one o'clock high," called Ray.

I saw the distinguishing identification of the 34th Bomb Group on the tails of the ships ahead. The front halves of all the vertical stabilizer of our tail assemblies were painted red. We banked slightly, and I gave a little more throttle as we slid gingerly into our slot at the tail end of the low squadron. From that moment, Glen and I kept our eyes on the three-plane element ahead and above us.

There were four flights of three planes in each of the three squadrons of a group, plus a tail end Charlie. Every pilot, except for the three squadron leads, flew formation off the plane to his right or left wing. When the lead plane dropped its bombs, the wing crew bombardiers hit their bomb release switch. If the target was obscured by clouds, we bombed by radar and the same procedure was followed. Only the lead planes of the high and low squadrons had radar.

Keeping close formation was integral to the success of this and every mission. We flew as if we were glued together. Colonel William E. Creer, our group commander, was a stickler for tight formations. We knew that the Luftwaffe would try to pick off planes that became separated. The tighter the formation, the more difficult for enemy planes to penetrate a wall of five hundred and forty-six .50-caliber machine guns. And the closer the formation, the greater the concentration of bombs on the target.

"Navigator to pilot," Ray called in, "we are over the Channel heading 85 degrees to Germany, and climbing two hundred and fifty feet a minute."

We were climbing to our bombing altitude at thirty thousand feet, nearly six miles above the ground. Glen took over as we climbed east, flying through thick contrails caused by condensation from the exhaust of the engines of the planes in the groups ahead.

This was one of the few tactical missions we flew. The Eighth Air Force was a strategic air force. Our goal was to fracture the enemy superstructure—communications, factories, power generators, oil refineries, and railroad marshaling yards way behind enemy lines— unlike the missions of the Ninth Tactical Air Force. The Ninth Air Force consisted of A-20s, B-26s, and B-25s, all twin-engined bombers. They provided direct support to the advancing Allied ground forces, attacking enemy troops, vehicles, railroads, and trains—anything that moved.

"Navigator to crew," Ray called in, "we're about twenty minutes from the I.P!" The Initial Point was the predesignated spot where the bombers would start their bomb run to the target. The route was often complicated, designed to avoid German defenses or deceive enemy radar about our true intentions. On reaching the I.P., the zigzagging and deceptions were over with and we headed straight for the target.

"Bomb doors open," our bombardier called, and I could feel the drag, the air resistance from the bomb bay doors hanging down from the belly of the plane. I moved throttles forward to compensate for the drag. Our visibility cleared and our bombardier was able to see the target on the ground. "Bombs away!" he shouted into the intercom while pressing the toggle switch. I had to strain to keep formation when over a ton of weight suddenly left the aircraft. The lead plane banked to the right and dropped its nose to pick up speed to move away from the target as quickly as possible. When the element lead moved, we moved. If we didn't, the planes above could settle right down on top of us. I was warned that had happened to other bombers.

Ray called in, "New heading. 260 degrees almost directly west to the base." And then Glen made a crew check. All voices were now clear, confident, even a bit bold.

The following day, *The Stars and Stripes* printed this account of the raid on Metz:

THIRTEEN HUNDRED HEAVIES POUND METZ

Halting temporarily the strategic bombing of industrial objectives in Germany, more than thirteen hundred 8th Air Force Fortresses and Liberators escorted by over five hundred Mustang fighters yesterday turned the crushing weight of their bombardment against targets in the Metz area in France in tactical support of General Patton's drive.

Not since the Normandy breakthroughs at St. Lo and Caen has tactical air support been used in such great strength. Fourteen U.S. bombers and nineteen fighters were lost, but some of these were believed to have landed in friendly territory. Of the forty-two 8th fighters reported lost in Wednesday's operation, nineteen have been reported safe.[6]

This had been our first mission; for us, fortunately, a "milk run" with virtually no enemy action. We headed back over the Channel. Off the left wing we could see the cliffs of Dover, steep and unforgiving, but a welcome sight and landmark. Finally, over the base, the lead element of the lead squadron peeled off, and as the others followed, they took two left turns to the downwind leg and then a third and fourth into the landing approach.

As we touched ground I believe the entire crew shared my sense of pride and relief at getting our first mission under our belt. As we pulled into our hardstand, Bruce Sothern gave us a thumbs up. We locked the brakes, cut the motors, collected our gear, and Glen and I eased ourselves down the escape hatch, dropping freely to the ground. The Red Cross wagon was there and the girls handed each of us a shot of whiskey. I gave mine to one of the guys who looked like he needed it the most. My stomach was too tight to take it.

My officers and I were taken to a small debriefing room where Intelligence asked us questions about the mission. Each officer reported separately. Intelligence was interested in the accuracy of the bombing from our perspective, short of receiving reconnaissance photos. At other debriefings, Intelligence would ask us about the accuracy of the flak in the target area and the response of the German fighters.

Afterwards, Ray and I were talking about the mission, and he told me that as we were flying over the target, we flew so close to the element leader that at one point he looked up and thought he could pat the other plane's ball turret gunner on the butt. We had slid in between two planes where we weren't supposed to be. Ray said his feet were hanging out of our plane to slow us down. I guess it worked, and we were still alive. That could easily have been a mid-air collision, luckily it was just a close call.

Ray and I walked back to our hut. On the way, we checked the crew list for the next day. We were on stand down, and relieved. I looked around the hut and noticed that the officers from the other crew were writing letters home. That seemed to be standard operating procedure. They had already completed several missions. I chatted with Ed, co-pilot for Lieutenant Davis. (We shared the hut with Davis and his officers.) Ed's cot was next to mine. I had just learned that he was from Chicago and I mentioned that I had spent last Easter in Evanston, with my cousins. He had no interest in talking. I was about to tell him my mother was born there, but thought better of it. Ed was writing a letter home, and it was clear that the last thing he wanted was to be distracted.

The next morning, a sergeant stood at my bedside with a flashlight in my eyes. It was 5:00 A.M. I sat up with a jolt. "You're operational, Ed." He had called me Ed. He had the wrong body. Ed was flying today with another crew to make up for a mission he had missed a few weeks before when he was sick. He wanted to get back in sync so he could complete his tour of duty with his own crew.

In the late afternoon, I walked over to chat with Bruce Sothern. He was standing on the tarmac waiting for the bombers to return from the mission. Bruce always wore an Air Corps coverall, the collar up around his neck, and a baseball cap. He was a quiet guy who projected confidence. Minutes later, a stream of B-17s approached the air base. Off in the distance, a plane was shooting red flares and heading straight for the runway. One engine was out and its plexiglass nose was smashed in. The other planes were told to circle until this damaged plane cleared the area. The pilot made a nice landing and the waiting fire trucks had a breather. The last of the three squadrons came in, but two of the planes peeled off to land quickly. As they did, each shot off one red flare indicating injured aboard. I noticed Bruce was distracted. He was counting the returning planes. "I think one is missing," he said.

I returned to my hut where it was deadly quiet. Lieutenant Davis broke the silence, "Ed's plane encountered heavy flak over the target. Crews reported seeing his plane go down in flames. No chutes." We were stunned, and sat in silence for a few moments. I walked over to Davis, his navigator, and bombardier to tell them how sorry we were.

Minutes later, a sergeant came into the hut, stripped Ed's bed, and placed his uniform on the bare mattress. He opened the footlocker and asked Davis if he or any of his crew wanted to go through Ed's belongings. No one wanted to do that. The sergeant pulled photos, stationery, and clothes from the trunk. I left the hut, walked outside, and motioned to the other guys in our crew to follow, and they did so without a word.

The stars filled the sky, and the galaxy seemed to reach out to us. There was still beauty in the world. As we walked around, I kept an eye on the door of the hut. After the sergeant left with his arms full of Ed's possessions, it was time to go back in. I looked at Ed's bed— the mattress was bare—a stark reminder of the frailties of life. The following day I couldn't stand it any longer. I folded Ed's cot and moved it against the wall.

Many times, I have thought of Ed and the many brave, young men who flew from their air base in the morning and never made it back.

(Map by Paul J. Pugliese. From *A Wing and A Prayer* by Henry H. Crosby. Harper Collins Publishers, 1993.)

THE RETURN

Twenty-one went out this morning
And the sun was in my eyes
As I watched them circle round
Before they vanished in the skie.

Twenty-one went out this morning
And the sunlight caught their wings
As they crossed the little thicket
Where a blackbird always sings.

Like birds into the morning
They flew I know not where
But small and secret in my heart
All day I've held a prayer.

Twenty-one went out this morning
Riding splendid thru the sky
But still there is no sign of them
Though soon the day will die.

Then suddenly thru time and space
There's sunlight on a wing
And above the beating of my heart
I hear an engine sing.

The sun still goes on shining
But my world grows dark with fear
For twenty-one went out this morning
But only seventeen are here.

—Beryl Miles

4

Assignment:
To Hell and Back

—◦•◦—◆—◦•◦—

November 25, 1944. The 34th Bomb Group was scheduled to fly, and by 5:30 A.M. all officers had gathered in the briefing room. I sat on the hard wooden bench with more than a hundred and fifty guys, each of them tense and nervous. The briefing room was filled with an aroma of soap, shaving lotion, and body sweat that seeped from the necks of our opened, fleece-lined jackets.

"Ten-shun!" the sergeant began the meeting, and our spines went stiff. Colonel Creer walked into the room and addressed his bomb group. He was standing on a slightly elevated platform in front of us. "Good morning gentlemen. Our mission is a tough one. It is aimed at the engine which drives the German war machine. I'll turn this over to the major who will brief you."

The curtains parted, revealing a floor-to-ceiling map of western Europe. Tape was pinned on the map indicating our routes to the target and back. The major continued, "Merseburg is in the southeastern part of Germany. It has the largest concentration of synthetic oil plants in the country." There was a hush from the officers, as if some hidden blow had knocked the wind out of us. We knew Merseburg would be a tough run. There was no target more dreaded by the Eighth Air Force than Merseburg. Four hundred and ninety antiaircraft guns were in the area to protect the oil plants, and three hundred and eighty more would be firing at us as we approached the target. Merseburg had the largest concentration of antiaircraft in Germany and I anticipated flying through black clouds of exploding shells.

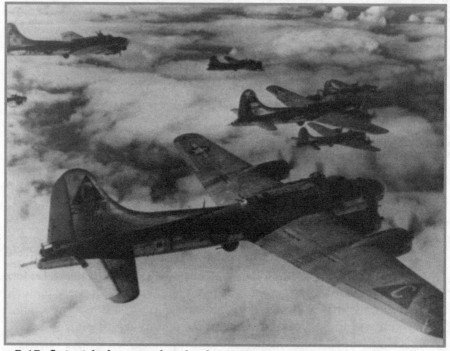

B-17s fly in tight formation for a bombing mission over Germany.
(Courtesy of Squadron/Signal Publications)

At the end of our briefing, we synchronized our watches. It was critically important that we conduct every mission with precision. We stepped outside and guys lit up cigarettes, puffing madly as we waited for our ride to the hardstands. I knew I'd smell of Lucky Strikes for hours.

This was our third mission, and we were still new to all of this, but we were flying with a group of seasoned pilots. Fortunately, the weather was clear on take-off. Once we saw the green flare from the tower, it was our signal to go. Our propellers fluttered, began to spin, and then settled into a throaty roar. One by one, the ships crept from their hardstands. Up ahead, I could see the vapor trails of hundreds of other bombers. At least we were not alone.

When we reached a cruising altitude of 27,000 feet, Glen made a routine crew check. Everyone was accounted for and the temperature was noted: minus forty-two degrees centigrade. War correspondent Walter Cronkite flew several missions with the Eighth Air Force and said it was impossible for reporters to take notes above twenty thousand feet because the bitter cold froze the lead in their pencils. Cronkite described a bomb run as an "assignment to hell."[7]

The B-17 handled well, but flying in tight formation was exhausting, especially in heavy flak. We were flying wingtip to wingtip with our wing tucked inside the one in front of us. The strategy was to hug the plane whose wing you were flying off. That would discourage enemy planes from diving through the formation.

We approached the target and up ahead, just two and a half minutes away, the sky seemed to be painted black with flak. Hundreds of antiaircraft shells exploded before our eyes, forming a dense carpet of explosive bursts that hovered in the air. We braced ourselves for the worst.

"Bombardier to crew. Six minutes to I.P." Pause. Silence. "Two minutes to I.P.," called our bombardier.

"Heavy flak ahead," I called into the intercom. "Here we go guys!"

"Okay," I thought, "Let's get this damn thing over with." I fixed my eyes on the ship off my wing and began humming one of my favorite hymns: "*A mighty fortress is our God . . .*" As the noise of the exploding shells grew louder, the plane shuddered and shook. Concussive blasts rocked the cockpit. Outside in the sky I saw sudden flashes of red turn into vicious clouds of black. We forged through other clumps of smoke and flak from shells that had exploded just seconds ago. I kept humming. I felt the presence of the Lord, and I put myself in his hands. I had total faith.

"Bomb bay doors open!" the bombardier yelled, and a swirl of cold air blasted through the plane. The noise of the explosions was now deafening as flak burst on all sides. I clenched my teeth, and thought, "Hang in there! Come on, drop those damn bombs!"

Then came the command we were waiting for: "Bombs away!" Our plane bounced up as the bombs were released. The whole group surged upward as a rain of 500-pound bombs poured to the ground below. The lead plane immediately banked to the right and picked up speed to get out of this maelstrom of exploding metal. Moments later, we lost power in our number three engine, and then number four went dead. They had frozen and the props had run away and jumped their governors. I had to leave the formation as we started to lose speed and altitude. With only the port engines working I had to

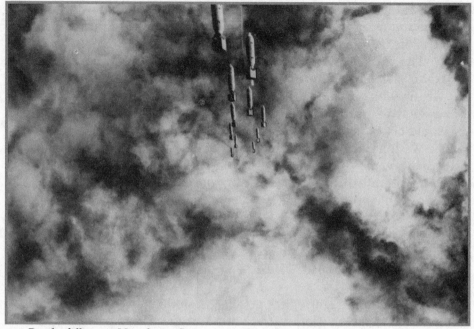

Bombs falling on Merseburg, Germany, in November 1944. (USAAF)

use all my strength to keep us straight. And once we were separated from the squadron, we were easy prey for the enemy, like a sitting duck. Strays like us were just what enemy fighters were waiting for. I pumped the throttles and prayed the engines would catch. It worked, and the power surged. I pushed the throttles forward to increase the manifold pressure—as much as I dared—and within a few minutes we were able to rejoin the pack.

"I have it!" I yelled to the crew.

I later learned that the lead plane saw us in trouble, and their bombardier kept a watchful eye on us. But now, thankfully, we were back with the flock, feeling a little less vulnerable. I tried to settle down, but nine pairs of eyes in the plane kept searching for German fighters. It was another four hours back to the English Channel, and we couldn't relax because enemy planes could attack us at any time during the return trip.

Our flight suddenly seemed strangely quiet, but lost in thought I kept flying until I felt a strong nudge on my right shoulder. Glen pointed to my mike which was now lying on my lap. I looked down and saw that there was a piece of shrapnel next to it. The rubber cord attached to the mike had been cut by shrapnel just an inch from my throat. No wonder it was all so quiet. Willie gave me a spare.

"Navigator to pilot. Navigator to pilot. Are you hurt?" called Ray.

"I'm okay," I responded.

Ray replied, "I thought you just said, 'I've had it!' and that you'd been hit."

Jack, our right waist gunner, called in, "Chuck, I've been trying to reach you. We have a large hole in the middle of the right wing, and so many holes in the waist, it looks like a sieve."

"Heck," Chuck Williams called in, "take a look at the hole on the left wing."

Our return trip took us south of our route to the target and then north across France. After passing those famous white cliffs, of which I was growing very fond, we landed cautiously and taxied to our hardstand. Our ground crew chief was alarmed at the extensive damage, and as he examined the plane he noted that two German 88mm shells had gone through both wings, somehow missing fuel tanks, aileron controls, and the steel frame of the wing assembly by inches. If any of these had taken a direct hit, it would have thrust the plane into a tailspin or caused an explosion that would have dropped us like a rock. There was not another part of the wing capable of withstanding such a large hole without causing fatal damage. The antiaircraft shells had traveled five miles straight up and through the wings of our plane. The shell had not been fused to go off on impact, but timed to explode at an altitude above us.

By that time the Red Cross wagon had pulled up and the girls were offering us shots of whiskey. Our ground crew chief informed me, "Chuck, we have counted sixty-two holes in the plane, and flak was found in the number two engine cover."

Just a single piece of shrapnel is enough to blow up an engine. One antiaircraft shell, exploding at the right time and the right place, will bring down a Flying Fortress. And just one piece of flak can kill someone instantly. Aside from the dozens of holes in our ship, we never knew how many shells just missed hitting us. I only know that a small piece of flak had just missed my throat, and if the rubber cord had not been there, I would have died.

THE ARROW AND THE SONG

I shot an arrow into the air,
It fell to earth, I knew not where:
For so swiftly it flew, the sight,
Could not follow it in its flight.

I breathed a song into the air,
It fell to earth, I knew not where;
For who has sight, so keen and strong,
That it can follow the flight of song?

Long, long afterward, in an oak,
I found the arrow still unbroke;
And the song, from beginning to end,
I found again in the heart of a friend.

—Henry Wadsworth Longfellow[8]

Sweating It Out—Did I Hear an Engine Roar?

———◦•◦———

December 1944   Christmas was three weeks away. For many of us, this was our first Christmas at an air base, and we were wishing we were elsewhere. Life at the base didn't change much, although I remember listening to the Armed Forces Network, which piped Count Basie, Louis Armstrong, Duke Ellington, and Glenn Miller tunes into the mess halls and clubs. But we could not get swept away with that alluring, sentimental rhythm, that smooth, brassy sound suggesting women and booze.

Occasionally, the Mendlesham air base had dances for everyone living at the base, and busloads of girls from nearby towns and villages arrived for the occasion. The only guys really excited about dances were those who worked on the base and never flew. The rest of us never had the luxury of feeling completely relaxed.

One December night, a dance floor was set up in the hangar. The place was packed. I got a beer and sat down with Ray. As the band struck up a Basie tune, Ray lit up a Lucky Strike. I looked across the hangar and saw some of the guys who worked at the base dancing steps I had never seen before. I wasn't in the mood to shuffle my feet, but my heart was warmed to see those guys cutting a rug on the floor. Still, no one toasted and no one celebrated anything, for that was bad luck. We were all a bit superstitious. In short time, I told Ray that I was heading back to the hut. He couldn't believe I was leaving so early and exclaimed, "Alling, you don't get around much anymore!"

My shoulders shook and I laughed with Ray. As I left, I looked over my shoulder where a bunch of guys were dancing cheek to cheek with their girls to the soft, sentimental sounds of *The White Cliffs of Dover*.

On December 5, 1944, the Eighth Air Force flew a massive air strike on Berlin. Five hundred and fifty bombers hit industrial targets in the German capital and destroyed the Tegl Ammunition Plant in its northwest suburb. The bombers were accompanied by eight hundred P-51 Mustang and P-47 Thunderbolt planes, and shot down more than eighty German fighters. Bombs were dropped on Hitler's underground bunker, but since it was reinforced by twenty feet of cement Hitler survived.

As we flew back over the English Channel, we returned to the peaceful British landscape with its winding country roads, small streams, hedgerows, and modest stone walls that formed a tapestry of farm land where herds of cattle and sheep appeared as small dots in the distance. I often wondered what it was like for those who lived near an air base, where peace and serenity were interrupted by a stream of bomb groups making their way to and from the coast. To some residents, though, it evidently seemed a grand sight. Pat Smithers, a housewife who lived under the path of Eighth Air Force bomber streams, described their presence:

BOMBERS FROM BRITAIN

If you live in Sussex or Kent nowadays (or I suppose in a good many other counties besides), you know before getting out of bed and pulling aside the black-out if it's a nice day. A clear dawn has a new clarion—the deep and throbbing roar of hundreds of planes, outward bound. They may be sailing high towards the coast, flashing or shining in the light of the sun that's not yet up over the horizon. Sometimes they look white and as graceful as gulls against the blue; at others they look black and sinister as they come and go between the clouds. But the impressive thing—the thing that makes land-girls pause in their stringing of the hopfields and makes conductors of country buses lean out and look up from their platforms—the impressive thing is the numbers. Never in the Battle of Britain, in the days when the Luftwaffe was beaten over these fields and woods, did the Germans send over such vast fleets. Never were their bombers four-engined monsters, such as these of the Americans which go out in their scores and hundreds. Sometimes you will see one big formation coming, say from the north, others from the north-east, others from the west, all heading for a common rendezvous. Their courses often converge, and a stranger to the scene might hold his breath seeing the approach of disaster as the formations close in. At the moment when it looks as if they must collide, he sees with relief that they're at different heights; and they make a brief, fascinating cross-over pattern and sail on as easily as an express train flies over complicated points. As their roar fades with them, another rises until things on the kitchen mantelshelf tinkle and rattle as they catch the vibration. Up over the beechwoods on the hill, the leading formation of a second wave of heavies appears, followed by others and still others. Some days it will go on like this pretty well all day—not all heavies, of course, but twin-engined bombers of various kinds, fighter-bombers and fighters . . . They have an appointment abroad, and they're keeping it.[9]

On December 6, 1944, we were awakened at 4:30 A.M. By 5:30 I was sitting with my officers in the Briefing Room. The briefing officer pulled the curtain cord that uncovered the secret information for the day's mission and route. He spoke deliberately and clearly to a bunch of guys ready for orders. "We return to Merseburg," he announced. Those words were chilling. The thought of returning to Merseburg made me nauseous.

I've blocked so much of this mission from my mind that I cannot describe it. Ray remembered it better than I. Of course, his view was slightly different than mine as he saw everything from the nose of the plane. One thing I remember is that Ray never led us astray. He was always as dead on target as he is with his memory. Ray described it this way:

We flew from the air base at 6:55 A.M. and climbed steadily and cautiously through a stairway of clouds until we reached our assembly altitude of 10,000 feet. The clouds formed peaks and

Ray Baskin, navigator on the B-17 Miss Prudy.

valleys, mountains, cliffs and plateaus, some massive and motionless, and others wispy. We flew back and forth above the clouds in search of other planes in the 34th Bomb Group.

By 8:43, the lead plane of the 34th fired a flare to give its plane a visual identification. Now it was time to enter into formation. We flew out over Dover and crossed the French coastline at 10:07 A.M., and flew along with the high squadron to the Initial Point of the bomb run.

At 11:36, we arrived over the IP. Our squadron "uncovered" and we adjusted our altitude, flying at the same level to avoid being hit by bombs from other squadrons. (There had been accidents caused by bombs being dropped on our own planes below. I recalled an incident where a 500-pound bomb dropped, cutting the left horizontal stabilizer off of a B-17 during a bomb run.)

Our bombardier for this mission was a member of the pool of crew from the base, as we still did not have a replacement for Mal. We sat back to back in the nose of the plane with a flak suit held in front of each of us. His primary responsibility was to hit the toggle switch when he saw the lead's bombs fall. I had then logged our position over the target.

In the distance, we saw the flak that surrounded the target across the city of Merseburg. Below us were the hundreds of antiaircraft guns that had been firing shells into the sky ever since we entered Germany. The P-51s followed us to the concentration over Merseburg and then broke off to circle around to the other side, waiting to escort us home. Our Little Friends were to stay away from the antiaircraft guns in the target area. I watched them circle near the IP waiting patiently for us to all return home with them. All the P-51s waited with the exception of one.

Willie watched the P-51 fly with us into the flak. He must have been a young, inexperienced pilot, devoted and overly enthusiastic. Then I heard Willie scream, "No!" and I looked out the window. The P-51 took a direct hit from flak and exploded off our left wing. The spirited plane was trying to protect us and never should have come so close.

Willie closed his eyes for a moment. A second later, he opened his eyes to a sudden flash of red light—the center of a shell burst within a few feet of our plane. The sky was so thick with flak that it was dark all around us. This was truly terrifying. All we could do was hope for the best and pray. I thought luck was on our side or that God was with us. I know that Willie bet on God. So did Chuck Alling.

By 11:47 A.M., we dropped our bombs. We were flying at 27,000 feet at a ground speed of 262 knots. It was minus forty-two degrees centigrade in the plane. At 12:51, below us en route to England, a P-47 was buzzing a German train with his guns blazing; at 1:31, small towns set off smokescreens impeding our visibility below; at 1:38, we passed seven miles south of Koblenz, Germany, and had descended to 23,000 feet; and at 2:58, we crossed the French coastline, landing back in England at 3:50 P.M. The mission had lasted for eight hours and fifty minutes. It was our seventh mission, and I was convinced we would never finish ten.

During the war the Eighth Air Force hit Merseburg sixteen times. As American troops overran southern Germany, Frederick Graham, correspondent with *The New York Times*, reported on the destruction of the city. The following is an excerpt from his article published on April 20, 1945:

Of the hundreds of bombed out cities, industrial plants, railway yards and airfields one sees while touring Germany in a jeep, perhaps none is as strong and unanswerable argument for strategic bombing as the sprawling heap of wreckage that used to turn out 600,000 tons of gasoline annually at the Leuna Works, Merseburg, Germany. Once Germany's largest synthetic gasoline and oil plant, it is the biggest junk heap I have ever seen. It has been completely ruined. Originally it had been an orderly mass of thousands of overhead and underground pipes and power lines and pipes ranging in diameter from an inch to six feet.

Scores of tanks, boilers and condensers tilt at crazy angles or look like giant sieves. Miles and miles of railway tracks and paved roads used to crisscross the whole plant, but they are now blown out or covered with wreckage. The plant employed 10,000 workers before the Air Force hit it first on May 12, 1944. From then on this complement was augmented by 4,000 more workers whose only job was to repair the plant after the aerial attacks.[10]

December 12, 1944   We flew our eighth mission, hitting the railroad marshalling yards in Darmstadt, just southeast of Frankfurt. Photographs indicated we had destroyed heavily loaded rolling stock and railroad repair facilities. The raid was a success. That was the one hundredth operational mission of the 34th Bomb Group.

The following day, Captain Brophy, the 7th Squadron operations officer, approached me on the base and led me into his small, sparse, and unassuming office. I didn't know what I was doing there. Unable to imagine what he wanted to talk about, I stood in silence in front of his desk until he walked up to me and placed his hand on my shoulder. "Alling," he said, "it is our squadron's turn to nominate the next crew in the Bomb Group for lead crew, and we've selected your team."

"Captain Brophy," I answered, "I am honored."

Brophy talked with me about the responsibilities of a lead pilot and explained that lead crews flew thirty missions, five less than other crews. With time off in between missions, however, it would take us a bit longer to complete our tour. Brophy also explained the risks involved. Lead crews were the most vulnerable target; Germans knew that the lead planes carried radar for navigation and bombing purposes. If the Germans were able to knock out the lead plane, they broke the group formation. Brophy finished with a warm smile. "Why don't you talk it over tonight with your boys and let me know. And by the way, congratulations Alling!"

That was a hell of an honor, and before I talked with anyone I wanted to find my friend, Lieutenant Davis. Already a first lieutenant, Davis was senior to me, and I had been sure he was next in line to be tapped for lead pilot. For some reason, I got the nod. I wanted to tell him in person before I told my crew; I didn't want him to hear the news from anyone else. We walked outside together and talked alone. True to his nature, he took it in stride and offered me encouragement, although I suspect that it was difficult news for him to take.

That evening, Glen, Ray, and I went over to the non-commissioned officers' barracks and sat down to talk it over with the guys. I explained the changes and the risks. Jack Brame was the first to speak, "You know, we're not surprised by this news and we're with you all the way."

"OK guys. Then, let's go! We'll have our own plane soon," I assured them.

We would now join other lead pilots and their crews—respected and accomplished pilots like Perry, Richardson, Daniels, and Sain, to name a few. I admired and respected these guys. Each had flown more missions than I. Captain Brophy assigned us a crackerjack bombardier, Bill Wright, and radar navigator, Mort Narva. Both had already flown with other crews.

William L. Wright was a native of Malden, Massachusetts, and raised in Florida. He was twenty-four when he was assigned to my crew. Bill was the kind of guy everyone respected. In his junior year in high school, he had received two college scholarships, but once his twin brother joined the military, Bill followed suit. He signed up for the Army Air Corps Cadet program and went to Ellington Field in Houston and then on to graduate from bombardier school in Midland, Texas. In September 1943, he married his hometown sweetheart, Nell. She had driven his Ford convertible all the way from New Smyrna Beach, Florida, to his base at Midland, Texas and never left his side.

By the time Bill was assigned to fly with us he had already flown eight missions with another B-17. On their first mission to Merseburg, the plane was forced to land in a field near Liege, Belgium. Bill and the rest of the crew found protection in the hands of sympathizers in the Belgium town of Gymmeppe, just liberated by the Allies. During their first night there, the Germans counter-attacked, recaptured the airfield and destroyed the hospital nearby. Shortly after, the Allies moved in with greater force, pushing the Germans back. Once Gymmeppe was freed again, Bill and his crew were flown in a C-46 back to the Mendlesham air base.

Mort I. Narva was from Newark, New Jersey, where his family owned a chain of shoe stores. Mort was twenty-three when he joined us. Married and a senior at the University of Pennsylvania when the Air Corps called him to active duty, Mort was a quiet, low-key guy. He loved cigars and sweets. Brophy remarked that Narva's wife had often sent him supplies of cookies and that in no time we should have our own stockpile of sweets.

As lead crew, we had to make other changes in order to allow for a command pilot to sit in the co-pilot's seat. Glen, my co-pilot, was to serve as an observer in the tail of the plane, sitting in our tail gunner's seat replacing George Rumbaugh. Glen would provide an extra set of eyes for the command pilot and relay information about the status of the squadron and the bomb group. The turret was soon to be replaced with a radar dome. Both George, my tail gunner, and Ward Yarborough, my ball turret gunner, were assigned to other bombers. We shook hands, said goodbye, and I wished them luck with their next assignment.

Captain Brophy offered Glen the choice of joining another crew as co-pilot or staying with us. Fortunately, he opted to stay even though sitting in the rear of the plane was not what he had ever wanted or planned to do. But we had been together from the start and Glen wanted to complete his tour of duty with us. While his new role seemed diminished, it was an important task and we trusted Glen for his astute capabilities and accuracy.

I had great respect for Glen, and in the eight missions that we had flown together, I knew that he and I thought as one. I remembered the times he helped save our lives or helped get us out of a jam. I thought of the times he'd look at me and I knew exactly what he was thinking. We trusted each other, and we knew that our crew depended on us working together. His departure might have had a terrible impact on our morale, just when we needed him most.

A few days later, we were assigned a new plane, this one ours for the duration. This was the plane we named *Miss Prudy*. I stepped on the tarmac to take a look. She was a beautiful silver fortress that had flown just a handful of missions, and I felt she was capable of flying us safely through many more. I walked up to her, hoisted myself through the escape hatch, climbed inside and sat in the pilot's seat. Speaking softly, even though no one was within ear shot, I whispered, "Okay, Prudy, we need you now more than ever. Please stay with me. Please watch over us."

I found a sergeant who worked in the bomb depot who had studied at an art school in the States. On the nose of the plane he

The Miss Prudy, *named for pilot Charles Alling's sister who had died shortly before he was sent overseas.* (USAAF)

painted a picture of a girl and wrote Prudy's name underneath. The beautiful portrait showed her facing forward, her hair flying back with the wind. *Miss Prudy* was now distinguished and ready to join forces with the other lead ships in the 34th.

For two weeks, we trained intensively for lead crew. We flew simulated bombing runs near the air base. Bill was assigned to practice dropping hundred-pound sacks filled with sand, one at a time, at precise locations. There was a smoke bomb in each of the group of sand bombs that released on impact so Bill knew exactly where the bombs landed—as did the group bombardier who flew with us to take a look. Bill's precision was remarkable.

We practiced leading small groups of planes, making gradual maneuvers, banking just fifteen degrees, climbing and descending at a gentle rate as well. It was impossible to rack a four-engine bomber around like a P-47. Lead navigators had to factor that it took a B-17 eight minutes to complete a 360-degree turn, covering a circle eleven miles in diameter traveling on a fifteen degree bank at 150 miles per hour.

One day, as we practiced a wing assembly over the English Channel, I saw an oil tanker grounded on a rocky shoal off of Felixstowe. As we circled and gradually approached the tanker, I asked Bill to take a good, hard look. Bill replied that he didn't see anyone and that furthermore there were no rescue boats in sight. I called the radio operator on the emergency frequency, "May Day, May Day!" and with great excitement at this discovery, I described the scene below.

"I read you loud and clear. Stay with me a minute to check on this." Moments later the operator responded to our urgent inquiry, "Thanks, but that ship went aground three months ago."

The next day, Glen practiced landings and lead formation. We traded seats. I was Glen's co-pilot during these exercises. During one landing we approached the runway traveling too fast. The wheels hit the tarmac, and when *Miss Prudy* bounced back up I felt that my stomach had jumped into my mouth. I was surprised my co-pilot had become so rusty. Ray was amused, and yelled into the intercom, "Oxygen check!"

Glen was nearly speechless with embarrassment, but retaliated, "Just checking to see if you're paying attention!"

We savored those light moments, no matter how trivial or fleeting. They gave us a lift, and helped brace us for the sobering moments that would follow.

On our last day of lead crew training, a B-17 with the 18th Squadron crashed on the airfield. The pilot had been trying to avoid a mid-air collision in the group assembly, and had spun into a nose dive. A few hours later, we left for our final training run and flew over a charred mess of mangled metal where ten young men had perished.

We had completed our training, and were each given a two-day pass. Bill and I left for London. We boarded the army shuttle truck to the Ipswich railroad station that brought us into Paddington Station. We booked into the Reindeer Red Cross Club, dropped off our gear, and dressed in our new pinks—faded pink dress pants—with our new jackets and low cut shoes, and stepped out on the town.

We bought tickets for the comedy *Meet Mr. Victoria*. Midway through the first act, the air raid warning light flashed above the stage. The yellow sign indicated enemy planes were approaching and it was time to head for a bomb shelter. No one left his seat and the show went on. Minutes later, the red alert light came on. Everyone still remained seated and the play continued. Seconds later, there was an enormous crash outside the theater. The stage shook, our seats shook, and we ducked. Bill and I sat motionless, frozen in our seats while the play went on. We stayed through the final act. I did not recall meeting Mr. Victoria. I was too stunned at realizing that after all we had been through, the end could come on leave in a theater.

After the show, we walked toward Piccadilly Square. It was pitch dark as London was still under blackout rules. Less than a block from the theater, there was a large hole in the middle of the street. Firefighters doused the flames in the nearby shops and buildings. Shopkeepers examined the damage with flashlights while the police and soldiers searched for people trapped in the rubble. Crowds gathered and mingled everywhere.

We soon returned to the Red Cross Club. After a hot shower, we crawled in between white sheets and civilian wool blankets in a dormitory room with eighteen cots. At 4:00 A.M., Bill woke to a startling noise. An Eighth Air Force pilot in our room leapt from one bed to the next, and then over to the window. He then opened the blinds to the darkness of the night and jumped. Bill explained, "I think you slept through it all, Chuck, but you weren't the only one. I tried to help him but it was too late. He jumped out of the window and landed three floors down on a metal grate. He couldn't take it any more."

"You know, Bill," I said, "this could have happened to any one of us."

At times, I felt I had nerves of steel, but there were also moments when I felt as though my life was a delicate balance. It would be all too easy to lose it. How can anyone brace himself for the horrors of war? And if you think about it too much, you can hardly go on. I couldn't let thoughts such as those linger. If I did, I couldn't get my job done.

The next morning we walked around London, over to 10 Downing Street, and then we bought a few Christmas presents at Selfridge's Department Store and had them shipped back to the States. We jumped on a double-decker bus to stop by Westminster Abbey, and made a visit to the Grosvenor House Officer's Club, where hundreds of American soldiers and airmen stopped for a drink and a tea dance. We spent most of that evening in a smoke-filled room. Snowflakes fell softly on London's streets that night while our planes continued to drop bombs on German soil not far away.

In late 1944, the American and British armies stalled at the borders of Germany. The freezing, murky weather and shrinking hours of daylight also grounded the Eighth Air Force as often as not. But while the American army in the field coped with its first winter in northern Europe, the Germans were accustomed to winter operations, especially after their experiences in Russia. In addition, since their Luftwaffe had been badly weakened, they preferred to fight when the air forces on both sides couldn't fly, even if it meant losing the support of their own.

On December 16, 1944, a huge German offensive burst into the center of the American front in the Ardennes Forest of southern Belgium and Luxembourg. Two panzer divisions crushed the U.S. lines and pushed dozens of miles, forming a huge "bulge" in the front. For days snow fell continuously and bomb groups in England were socked in. Every hour that the Eighth Air Force remained grounded German tanks pushed farther through the Ardennes. Finally, after more than a week of frustration, the weather cleared.

December 24, 1944   The Eighth Air Force and the Ninth Air Force both soared into the skies in a massive combined strike to stem the German offensive. This mission was strictly tactical to aid the ground troops in the Battle of the Bulge. It was only a three hour mission to southern Belgium, and two sorties were flown on the 24th.

We were not assigned to fly that day and so it was our turn to sweat it out, waiting for the bombers to return to Mendlesham. Now I had an idea how tough it is for ground crews to wait—this was a test of patience that required a different kind of fortitude and endurance.

In the early evening, Ray and I walked outside and watched the bombers returning to the base. The weather had closed in again over much of England. A hundred and ten planes from the 1st Division were diverted to Mendlesham because their airfields, to our west, were socked in, and our base still had visibility. One after another, scores of formations, hundreds of four-engine bombers appeared off the horizon. When they flew overhead, their navigation lights, running lights, landing lights were all lit up. Red, green, and white lights sparkled in the sky, moving in a slow, definite pattern toward Mendlesham.

This Christmas Eve was described by Edwin Smith, the 34th Bomb Group historian:

> The spirit of Christmas remained intangible until a chill moment just at sundown on Christmas Eve. The sky had turned an ersatz purple and a group waiting on the ground for the planes to return from the mission saw scores of formations—hundreds of bombers—appear out of the horizon. They began to pass overhead . . . with a myriad of colorful lights from their navigation and running lights. The purple had almost faded and now from all parts of the sky multicolored rocket flares soared from the midst of the formation, curving upwards and down again, dying out as they fell earthwards, finding answer from the ground as flares were set off in reply. For several moments the realization that they were men and planes gave way to a mind picture of a vast, abstract

Christmas tree, beautifully trimmed in a pattern of moving lights invisibly guided through the dark infinity of dusk, huge and colorful, impressive. Then the mind's focus returned to the moment, the time, and the deeper significance that these were men and planes returned. The fanciful Christmas tree in the sky disintegrated. With roaring engines, the fortresses glided down onto the field, landed. But there was no more time for dreaming.[11]

Ray and I were mesmerized by this spectacular sight. "Stop day-dreaming, Ray!" and I nudged him jokingly. "Shape up!"

"I'm just dreaming of a white Christmas," he responded in a wistful voice.

More than one thousand airmen from other bomb groups landed at Mendlesham that Christmas Eve. They were thankful to be there, though anxious to return to their base in the morning, knowing they would be sleeping in their planes that night. Many came to the Officer's Club where food and booze were plentiful. I looked out the window from the club and saw a steady stream of planes still returning. Word was out that one pilot had just landed and taxied off the runway in the wrong direction. The control tower asked the pilot, "B-17, are you lost?"

"No!" he responded emphatically, "I need a drink! I'm heading to the Officer's Club!"

The late night Christmas Eve service was jammed, and it seemed that all our voices were muted as we sang "Silent Night" and "O Come All Ye Faithful." We were grateful to be alive. I thought about our countrymen who were POWs, and the many who had died. I barely heard the prayers muffled in the background, for my thoughts were three thousand miles away.

Christmas day was a nostalgic time for everyone, especially for the guys who were married. I gathered with my crew in our hut. We stoked the coal stove and opened our Christmas presents one at a time—savoring each moment, hoping it would last. We squirreled away our presents in our footlockers, except for one. Bill handed me a heavy, brown bag with a ribbon tied around it. I thought this was an unusually heavy present. I thought he had really gone out of his way to find something valuable. I opened the brown bag to find a small stash of coal.

We read our letters from home and friends stationed in Europe and the Pacific. My father sent clippings from *The New York Times* and *The Montclair Times* with communiqués on the Eighth Air Force. My family and Sonny Walker sent letters. I read them over and over again, nearly memorizing each one. I took my letters, tied them together, and stowed them away.

My uncle, Kenneth Alling, wrote a poem which I read to my crew on Christmas night.

To The Crew Of The Prudy K.

> *From one who should know*
> *Which way the winds blow*
> *We have heard that your show*
> *Is good, for any man's dough.*
>
> *We're proud of the crew of the Prudy K.*
> *Of the men who service her, o.k.*
> *Of the team which flies her from dark to day*
> *And they who send the bombs away.*
>
> *Merry Christmas, Happy Landings,*
> *Good luck and our best*
> *And may you always be,*
> *By the good Lord, most blessed.*

That night, I paused for a few moments and looked around at my crew. We were a group of guys who lived together, flew together, and fought together. We were a team joined at the hip. Each guy gave everything he had. My crew would say that they were just an ordinary bunch of guys, but I would say something quite different. I would say that I was surrounded by brave men whose accomplishments, I believe, were a part of the fabric of history.

Glen Banks, co-pilot

Jack Brame, gunner

Bill Wright, bombardier

Chuck Alling, pilot

The Crew of Miss Prudy

(All photos courtesy USAAF)

Mort Narva, radar navigator

Willie Green, crew chief

Chuck Williams,
gunner

Ray Baskin, navigator

Eddie Edwards, radio operator

The Journey

I go not where I will but must;
This planet ship on which I ride
Is drawn by a resistless tide;
I touch no pilot wheel but trust

That One who holds the chart of stars,
Whose fathom-lines touch lowest deeps
Whose eye the boundless spaces sweeps,
Will guide the ship through cosmic bars.

My soul goes not a chosen way;
A current underruns my life
That moves alike in peace or strife,
And turns not for my yea or nay.

Not on the bridge, but at the mast,
I sail o'er this far-streaming sea;
I will arrive: enough for me
My Captain's smile and words at last.

—John T. McFarland[12]

6

Near Miss

——◦◦●◦◦——

At the end of 1944, Lieutenant General James H. Doolittle, commanding officer of the Eighth Air Force, gave an account of operations during the past year. The Mighty Eighth had released 430,000 tons of bombs on enemy territory and flown 1.7 million operational hours. His year-end message to the airmen extolled this contribution to the Allied war effort:

> The year 1944 was a significant one for those who have devoted themselves to the cause of freedom and justice throughout the world. . . . Here in the European Theatre, the Eighth Air Force fought with distinction. It contributed importantly to the Allied war effort and earned a place in history which time will not erase.[13]

January 10, 1945   Our first mission of the new year was to Cologne, Germany, located on the Rhine River, fifty miles west of Belgium, where Allied forces were still trying to push the Germans back out of Belgium. This was our first mission as a lead plane. We were the lead plane of the low squadron.

On our approach to Cologne, Bill looked below to be sure all planes were clear of one another for the bomb run. Everything was fine. "Bomb bay doors open!" Bill called. Seconds later, just before we dropped our bombs, Bill looked at the group ahead of us and saw a B-17 settle-down on top of another. As its props chewed up the plane underneath, the tail below cut through the fuselage of the plane on top. Both planes exploded simultaneously leaving behind scattered remains and ashes of twenty young Americans trapped inside the inferno. That was a horrific sight, but we had to stay focused. We dropped our bombs and watched the planes of our comrades burn in hell. Pieces of metal ripped apart, tearing through corridors in the sky, falling on enemy territory.

Upon our return to Mendlesham, the Red Cross met us at the hardstand with hot chocolate and whiskey, and we were whisked away to our debriefing. Intelligence took a look at the photos, and we were given our rating for this mission: "good."

By the end of the war, Cologne was the second most heavily bombed city in Germany. In 1942 it had been the first to receive a "Thousand Bomber Raid" by the RAF's Bomber Command. After that, its strategic location on the Rhine, and later, its proximity to the front, had made it the target of many subsequent missions. Cologne nearly ceased to exist, with the odd exception of a great lovely cathedral that remained intact, pointing to the heavens in the center of all the devastation. Some claimed the cathedral remained unscathed because of bombing accuracy. I was not certain of that. Wags said that it survived only because Allied bombers used it as an aiming point. Whether it was accuracy, inaccuracy, or luck, the fact remains that this beautiful structure still stood at the end of the war.

January 20, 1945   At 4:30 A.M. I woke to the whistling wind swirling around the hut, and then the deliberate, determined footsteps of a sergeant. "You're operational! Out of the sack men!" he announced. He stood in the open doorway, bringing with him the familiar morning freeze. This was another cold, brisk day; one of those days the chill penetrates your bones. No one stirred, and so he followed with another announcement, "This is war, men! Move your butts!" The sergeant left in stony silence. Reluctantly, we rose from our covers and in less than a minute we were dressed in flying gear. I slung my heavy, fleece-lined, leather flying jacket over my shoulder and walked through the biting cold to the washroom, where I doused my face with cold water and soap.

Outside, an army truck was waiting for us. We jumped in and sat on damp, unforgiving wooden benches, huddled under a heavy tarpaulin, seeking shelter and protection from the falling snow.

Someone tapped on the side of the truck, and with a jolt we were on our way to the mess hall for breakfast—artificial eggs, rolls, and instant coffee. We went through the dining motions quite mechanically. If you wanted salt or pepper, you pointed. If nothing happened, you issued a mumbled command. There were no conversations, no kind or thoughtful words. Guys were tense and anxious and some may have wondered if their time was up, but I couldn't dwell on those thoughts. I was watching the time, as I could not be late for the briefing.

I entered the briefing room with other pilots and officers of the Bomb Group and sat next to my four officers: Glen, my co-pilot; Ray, our navigator; Bill, the bombardier; and Mort Narva, our new radar navigator. We were flying lead of the low squadron on this mission, so Glen was able to resume his position in the cockpit instead of making room for a command pilot. None of us realized at that moment how fortunate we were to have him back there.

Colonel Creer, our Group commanding officer, explained the purpose of the mission and bid us "Good luck and God bless." The briefing officer drew back a curtain that revealed a wall-size map of western Europe that contained secret information for this mission. A red tape was placed on strategic locations forming aerial highways to the target that would also steer us clear of German antiaircraft installations. The map indicated a control point where the 34th Bomb Group was to meet up with P-51 fighter escort planes that would fly with us and provide protection from the Luftwaffe fighters. Other critical markings on the map included our Initial Point of the bomb run, where we were to turn toward the target. After we had dropped our bombs, we were to meet at the Rally Point and follow our assigned route home. If we had to abort the primary target, a secondary target was predetermined.

Next, Intelligence officers briefed us on the expected status of enemy aircraft and intensity of flak. Then weather officers provided detailed reports on weather conditions for the eight-hour mission to Germany and back.

We had our orders, gathered our parachute packs, and met up with the army trucks that delivered us to our B-17 Flying Fortress. We jumped into the truck where we were joined by the other members of my crew: Willie, the crew chief; radioman Eddie; and gunners Jack and Chuck. All over the air base, trucks moved slowly and cautiously, carrying crews to their bombers. Everyone worked quickly and quietly. Everyone knew his job.

Our ground crew chief and his dedicated assistants were patiently waiting for us at the hardstand, after working into the night to keep *Miss Prudy* in good shape. The ground crew chief seemed pensive and concerned; his eyebrows were crinkled and laden with snow.

We stepped out of the truck and climbed into our plane. Glen and I nervously settled into our bucket seats, put on our headsets and parachute harnesses. There was no time for small talk. We were all business. Glen led us through the routine checklist and crew check. My heart was beating rapidly, and I took a deep breath of cool air. Glen announced we were ready to proceed: "All accounted for. Ready to go." We waited impatiently yet reluctantly for the green flare from the control tower down the runway—a signal that it was time to start our engines.

This was our thirteenth mission. I was feeling a bit superstitious, also anxious about flying in the snowfall with poor visibility. I felt something inauspicious looming over us like a dark cloud. I was dreading the thought of climbing into the clouds with hundreds of

Some of the ground crew for Miss Prudy. (USAAF)

planes flying together in the "soup" in a forty by sixty mile area. This morning six hundred bombers from sixteen bomb groups were to assemble over England and fly in tight formation with the lead squadron in the front, the high squadron above and to the right, and the low squadron below and to the left. If every navigator and pilot followed the take-off and assembly process perfectly, there would not be a single mishap. But on a day like this, that was asking a lot.

At 6:15 A.M. the green flare shot up from the control tower. "Starting engines," I announced over the intercom. We were the lead bomber of the low squadron, and the third ship to take off. I looked out the window and our ground crew chief was standing on the tarmac below. He gave me the thumbs up and I nodded back. He walked away with his head down.

I released the brakes and pushed the throttles forward ever so slowly, but just enough to get our Flying Fortress in motion. She was carrying three tons of bombs and 2,780 gallons of gas. Within four minutes, we were in take-off position. I looked down the runway. Visibility barely reached one hundred yards, and with every minute it diminished. Snowfall of this magnitude in Britain was unusual at this time of the year.

We crept along, slowly gained momentum, cleared the runway and started our climb. Every thirty seconds a B-17 took off behind us, until the entire 34th Bomb Group had flown from Mendlesham air base. Over the next four minutes, we continued our ascent through the clouds at 150 miles an hour. We were all quiet, knowing the departure into thick cloud cover was troublesome and a potential nightmare, but so far, so good.

At two thousand feet, I was stunned to see a B-17 just off my right wing heading directly toward our bow. Instinctively I thrust the steering wheel forward to push down the nose to avoid impact. We came within a few feet of a mid-air collision. The tunnel of air rocked our plane as the other B-17 roared above. Our plane then started to plunge downward, gaining momentum every second. Snow plastered the windshield, and to our horror, we headed straight down toward the ground. All I could do to save our ship was pull back on the controls with all the strength I had. She wasn't able to break out of the dive. I knew we only had seconds left. Then Glen jammed both his feet against the instrument panel and hauled the steering wheel up against his chest. Now I felt our plane miraculously responding—she shuddered and shook with a thunderous noise as gravity finally released its terrifying grip. Using every ounce of strength and power, she leveled off and gradually climbed back into the clouds. Within ten minutes, we had returned to two thousand feet, back where we began.

There was a deafening silence on board our ship. My knuckles were white and locked onto the steering wheel. My body broke into a sweat, only to cool rapidly in the freezing temperature inside the plane. I looked at Glen. Beads of sweat were dripping from his forehead. We didn't say anything above the roar of our engines, we just looked at one another wondering how we had made it through. I admired Glen's ability to respond so quickly under duress, and later told him so. Neither one of us alone could have done it.

It was time to check in with the crew. "Pilot to bombardier. Pilot to navigator . . ." So far everyone was checking in, a bit shaky, but in one piece. "Pilot to right waist gunner. Pilot to waist gunner." Silence. Jack Brame failed to check in. I called him on the intercom, "Jack, do you hear me?"

"Chuck, there's something wrong with my leg. It was caught underneath the walkway and it's twisted."

"Are you okay, Jack? Are you in pain?" I asked.

"A bit," he said, "but don't worry about it."

We continued to climb up to seven thousand feet toward the assembly point directly over the town of Felixstowe. Willie Green, standing in the top gun turret just beyond me, called in over the intercom to tell me that the tip of the right wing was bent upward.

I asked Glen to check on Jack and assess the damage to the wing. Glen reported that Jack had twisted his leg and that he needed immediate attention. And he said our right wing was damaged and thought we must have hit a tree or telephone pole. I radioed the base, asking permission to abort the mission. The operations officer agreed and instructed us to circle above the clouds until we received landing instructions because there were still hundreds of planes in the clouds waiting to break through and assemble.

Our landing was challenging, given the structural damage and our full load of bombs. A rough landing could cause a bomb to unhinge, forcing the bomb bay doors open with its release on the runway. But somehow we managed a safe landing and taxied slowly to the hardstand, making every effort to avoid potholes on the way. With our ground crew waiting for us, I shut off the engines and jumped out of the plane.

It was time to assess the damage, the extent of which I hadn't imagined. A foot of our wing had been sheared off—most likely by the branch of a tree. Green, raw wood was jammed into the wing, and fence wire was snagged in the belly of the plane. Clearly we had come several feet from hitting the ground. Our ground crew chief looked at me: "If you had lost another few inches you would not be standing here." A half a second, even less, was all the time we'd had left in that dive. I loved this plane. Somehow she had safely carried us back to the air base.

The operations officer drove up in his jeep and announced there was another plane waiting for us and her engines were running. He was anxious that we fly until he noticed the strain on our faces and the damage to our plane. He took a look at Jack carted away on a stretcher and thought it was best that we take a rest.

This near-miss can still make me break out in a chilly sweat, although some of my crew had a different reaction than I. Both Ray and Bill were certain that their end had come, but they seemed at peace with it. Bill thought of one thing during our descent. He imagined his life would be remembered in a brief obituary in his hometown paper. "That's God's honest to goodness truth!" he claimed.

Ray said he felt resolved during those moments. "You know, my whole life passed before me and I was prepared to die. For some reason, I was completely relaxed."

In those few, terrifying moments, I didn't think of anything meaningful or philosophical. I just knew that Glen and I had to somehow get out of the mess. For an unexplained reason, both Bill and Ray experienced that sense of calm—a strange phenomenon, I am told, just moments before dying. But this was not our time to die; it was another close call, and I was certain there would be many more to come.

SORROWS ARE AS STORMS

When storm clouds gather on a sunny day
And quickly rush across the land and sea,
With thunder cloud and lightning's brightest ray;
They soon are past and leave the heavens free
From dark and sombre hues that hide the light;
And when the cold and whistling blasts do blow
A crewing storm from east to west with might
And days on end the swirling mists hang low;
Yet will the gate of heaven's sluiceway stop,
The clouds retreat with slow and angry pace,
A patch of blue, a beam of sunlight top
The last of these to clear the sky's blue face.
It's thus that sorrows smite the human heart;
Some long, some short, but all of them depart.

—Henry Russell Ames[14]

7

Merciless Hail

————•◦◆◦•————

*F*ebruary 3, 1945   At 3:30 A.M. a voice barked: "Gentlemen, you're operational! Now!" With winter's fewer hours of daylight we were kickstarted earlier in the morning. By 4:30 A.M. we were in the air on our way to Berlin. This time we were the lead ship in the high squadron.

The strategy behind the Eighth Air Force missions began at Pinetree, code name for the Eighth Air Force General Headquarters, located in a mansion in High Wycombe, near London. At Pinetree, the Eighth's high command worked from a priority list supplied by Supreme Allied Headquarters in London. Once a target was selected, Intelligence, Operations and Planning, and Supply began their work. By the time we were briefed for a mission, planning for the air strike had long been underway, with hundreds of hours invested in preparations.[15]

The mission this day was masterminded by General James Doolittle, commander of the Eighth Air Force, and planned as a "maximum effort." It was the largest air strike yet, involving forty-two bomb groups—a total of sixteen hundred B-17 and B-24 four-engine bombers accompanied by nine hundred P-47 and P-51 fighters. By the time the first bombers were over Berlin, the last were still crossing the English Channel on their way to Germany. Our targets were the government and military offices, railroad yards, and industrial plants in the city's center—an area of two square miles.

Ray recalled the tasks of a lead navigator on this mission:

> My desk was small and low to the floor. I sat on my parachute pack, and wore my parachute harness and Mae West lifejacket.

My feet rested on the cold floor; a thin strip of metal. Once the auxiliary power unit was cranked up, I had some light at my desk. I plugged in my heated suit and started plotting our course on the chart. Eventually, I felt warm and quit shivering from the cold and anxiety. I checked my oxygen, my parachute harness, sharpened my pencil, found my erasers and was prepared for combat—although I often wondered if I was ever ready.

After taxiing into take-off position, Chuck locked the brakes and revved up the engines, one at a time to maximum manifold pressure. When they checked out fine, he released the brakes and slowly accelerated down the runway into the black, foggy drizzle. All I could do was sit there on my chute pack and wait to see if "Her Majesty" would fly. I thought, "If she doesn't fly, I am going to be part of a terrible mess in this Plexiglas nose."

Watching my airspeed indicator, I looked for 130 MPH, and at 125–130 MPH she would start to lift off. When Chuck hauled back, I knew she'd fly. Two or three minutes later, the aircraft gear and flaps were up. We were flying at 150 MPH and pointed towards buncher 19—a radio station. As we gained altitude, we flew from buncher to buncher until we saw the group lead. Once we were above the clouds, we slid into formation along with the other planes. Chuck maintained a 150 MPH indicated air speed and a climb rate of 250 feet per minute. It was frightening to see so many blue flames from the exhaust stacks of other aircraft so close. Often we were caught in the slipstream of other bombers which made our plane shudder and I'd shudder myself as I recorded another near miss.

I stayed busy trying to stay on the planned course to avoid the flak areas we had been briefed about. I would tell Mort, our radar navigator, what to look for on his radar chart; a river, a town or a railroad, and most of the time he found it immediately.

We changed headings frequently to avoid as much flak as possible. This made navigation more difficult with the lack of aids. Sometimes the heading changes were rather sharp. I tried to cut corners short to round out the turn since we were

limited to a fifteen degree bank. I learned early on that those
flak charts were not necessarily correct and we were shot at
regardless.

At the I.P., Bill controlled the aircraft to the target with
the Norden bombsight. If he was busy setting up the bombsight and looking for the target, I would help him once we
could see the ground. Usually we got the heaviest flak between
the I.P. and rally point where the aircraft re-formed into normal formation position. We tried to forget about the flak and
just plow on through. Bill and I had to focus on our jobs with
nothing but complete concentration. Our performance would
determine the success or failure of the mission; I had to line up
on the target, and he had to hit the target.

Just before reaching the target, a German fighter flew directly
through our squadron from the rear, and up in front of us to the left
whereupon his plane did a pirouette on its tail, like a ballet dancer,

Aerial war photograph of the bombs from Miss Prudy *hitting Berlin on
February 3, 1945.* (U.S. Army Air Corps)

and then exploded. We flew right through the mass of exploding metal, a piece of which tore into our right wing. Somehow, all the planes in our squadron survived as they flew through the remains of the German plane.

Our return home was smooth and Ray remembered our relief as we flew over the coast of England heading back to our base:

> Before the descent began, we took off our oxygen masks and lit up a fag. Even Chuck was known to light one up occasionally. Then he would peel off over the base, land, taxi, and shut down the engines. We dismounted through the escape hatch and thanked the Lord for watching over us. We had one less to go. The more missions we finished, the more we sweated each one; but after twenty missions, I started thinking, "Maybe we have a chance."

During the air strike over Berlin, the flak was heavy and accurate. Eighty percent of all bombers received some damage and nineteen went down. Any loss was tough to take, and it made me wonder when our time would be up. The damage to *Miss Prudy* from the exploding metal was significant; our left wing was hit about six feet from the fuselage. When we returned to the air base, our ground crew chief took a good look at the damage on the wing, and told us if that same amount of flak had hit the nose, things would be different. "You two guys," he said, pointing to Bill and Ray, "probably would not be standing here. If the flak had hit number two engine, a few feet on the other side, none of you would be standing here. *Miss Prudy* would have exploded." Another close call.

Berlin, like Cologne, suffered a devastating onslaught of bombs. The German Air Ministry received direct hits as did the government buildings surrounding it. The Reich Chancellory, Ministry of Propaganda, and Gestapo Headquarters were smothered under eighteen concentrations of high explosives. Five railroad stations were hit, and the Tempelhof marshalling yards, Tempelhof Airdrome, and the Deutsche Gas Works suffered serious damage. Estimates of civilian casualties ranged from minor to as many as twenty-five thousand dead. The raid was described as "record breaking, devastating and unprecedented."[16]

Josef Goebbels, who aside from being the Nazi Propaganda

Minister was gauleiter of Berlin, issued a standard order to the millions of refugees in Berlin forbidding them to leave the city. "After suffering terrible casualties in yesterday's great air attacks, the homeless masses are trapped in the still burning capital and must share whatever new disasters may befall it."[17]

Two weeks later, the following account of the February 3rd raid over Berlin was published in *The Stars and Stripes*. This dispatch was written by Herbe Granberg, correspondent for the *Aftonbladet*, a newspaper published in Stockholm. (Granberg was the first neutral correspondent to leave Germany since 1943.)

During the American bombing attack on Berlin on February 3rd, I sought safety in an underground railroad tunnel, one of Berlin's safest "shelters." Thousands of people stood in clusters or sat in overcoats along the massive concrete walls—grotesque in ghostly light.

The ground heaved, lights flickered. It seemed the concrete walls bulged, people scrambled about like frightened animals. A girl in a group of Russian laborers began to sing in mass. "Shut-up," somebody shouted, but the girl continued.

Then came the next load. Six or seven explosions right above us and a string further away. The light in the tunnel went out. We sat in the musky darkness. Some pocket torches were lit, but they proved useless in the cloud of chalky dust which came welling through the tunnel. It penetrated the eyes, the mouth, the nose and ears. People kneeled and prayed.

After ear-shattering blasts, there was silence. Air pressure increased in the tunnel and I held my mouth open to equalize the impact on the eardrums. A heavy bomb had crashed through the tunnel roof a hundred yards away. A wave of cold air followed the dust.

"Quit smoking," someone shouted in the darkness and several hysterical persons took up the cry. In the distance someone yelled for a doctor, but the clamber for help taken up by many voices was drowned out by the next wave of bombs.

The explosions shook the concrete structure. By the crash you could tell several bombs had pierced the upper floor of the elevated railway station. "For heaven's sake, stop it. Put an end to this insanity. Put an end to the war," a woman screamed. "Shut-up with that," broke in a man's voice. And a stir ran through the packed shelters.

Four more strings of bombs came down. Finally there was a lull, an expectation of the "All Clear." It was difficult to breathe. No one said much. Some were talking in low voices.

In the elevated station, the dead were all around. One man apparently had his lungs blown out by air pressure.

Hardly anyone rushing out of the tunnel paid attention to the dead. Everyone had his own troubles. In the square a hurricane of fire raged. Smoke and flames limited visibility to fewer than one hundred yards. I was blinded by smoke and soot.[18]

Newspaper reports described the enormity of the Berlin raid as providing leverage to Roosevelt and Churchill's bargaining position at the Yalta Conference on February 4. Joseph Stalin had to acknowledge the presence of American and British air power in his backyard.

Bill gave me his report of the Berlin raid, and his attitude differed markedly from the press reports of German reactions. "I intend to live forever, and so far I'm doing pretty well." And the next morning, true to his word, Bill was still alive. I wished I felt as positive as Bill, but that was hard, especially when the weather remained cold and chilly. And that day, the rain was incessant, steadily pounding the metal roof of our hut, creating a roar. I left for a few moments to be by myself, and went to the combat crew library where there were wall-sized maps showing every theater of operation. Colored pins and ribbons indicated the Allied lines. Plastic colored arrows showed our advances and identified the different army divisions. I picked up a novel and sank into a deep armchair. I looked up at the wall of colored pins, each blended into a rainbow of colors that blurred my vision, and I fell into a deep sleep.

I returned to the hut later that night. The next morning, Bill and I were the first to rise, so the job of fetching coal to warm the hut rested with us. Neither one of us could imagine lugging the coal back to our hut from the coal dump at the base. We stood together, peering out our window at a farm just beyond the border of the air base. And then we both had the same thought. We looked at each other, and without saying a word, grabbed the empty coal bucket and quietly left on our mission.

We climbed over the fence to the neighboring farm, walked over to the coal shed adjoining the farm house, and filled our bucket full of coal. Within moments, a small young boy appeared from around the corner. He was dressed in charcoal-colored overalls and a gray jacket. He stopped, glared at us and put his hands on his hips. "What are you doing?" he asked incredulously.

"We're getting some coal," we said, stunned that we needed to provide an explanation.

With as much outrage as he could muster, he replied, "Do you know whose coal that is?"

"No!" Bill said.

"That's the King's coal," he announced indignantly.

And with that Bill responded, also indignantly, "Well, the hell with the King!"

The perplexed and angry young lad responded with defiance, "And the hell with Babe Ruth!"

———•—◆—•———

February 14, 1945   We were briefed for Chemnitz, Germany, thirty-five miles southwest of Dresden, one of the country's industrial centers with machine tool and armament factories, and a network of railroad yards.[19]

It was estimated that the mission to Chemnitz would take nine hours. We were warned of bad weather and heavy clouds both on the way to and over the target, and this forecast proved to be accurate. Not far from the I.P., clouds came between us and the group lead. The group command pilot radioed us to have the squadrons break off and hit one of the targets of opportunity. My command pilot acknowledged the order, and we left for the city of Hof where we were to hit the marshalling yard.

Ray spoke to Bill and me on the intercom: "We have a tough one. Hof is not very far away. I'm going to put you immediately on a bomb run heading to the new target. Bill you're not going to have much time to find the target, but going west the weather should clear up enough for a visual run."

Minutes later Bill called in, "I can see the ground. Hof is up ahead a few moments away. Bomb bay doors open." Bill engaged the Norden bombsight, and he was in control of the lateral direction of

Handwritten: #12 "Hof" crab (Oak Leaf Cluster Mission) led Low Sqd. 5

SECRET   Mission of 14 February 1945
34 "A" Sq. LEAD (93 A Gp)

ASSEMBLY ROUTE:
Bu 23
A-0946   Southwold
B-1002   A- 0951
       B- 1007

Bu 19
A -0936   C 0934
B -0956   climb 0959

Ref. Base Wind 260 degrees, 70 knots
Ref. Base Alt. 22,000   Zero Hr. 0930
Gp Preceeding:
45 C Gp - Vampire Charlie (GG) - 3 min
Gp Following: (RY)
93 B Gp - Clambake Baker - RY-2 min

COMMUNICATIONS:

4 "A" Group	Hotshot Able	B	GG
4 "B" Group	Hotshot Baker	B	YY
4 "C" Group	Hotshot Charlie	B	RG
4 "D" Group	Hotshot Dog	B	RR
13 "A" Group	Fireball Able	B	YY
13 "B" Group	Fireball Baker	B	GG
45 "A" Group	Vampire Able	B	RG
45 "B" Group	Vampire Baker	B	RR
45 "C" Group	Vampire Charlie	B	GG
93 "A" Group			
34 "A" Sq	Clambake Able Lead	B	RR
34 "B" Sq	Clambake Able Hi	B	RR
34 "C" Sq	Clambake Able Lo	A	RR
93 "B" Group			
490 "A" Sq	Clambake Baker Lead	A	RY
490 "B" Sq	Clambake Baker Hi	A	RY
490 "C" Sq	Clambake Baker Lo	A	Py
93 "C" Group			
493 "A" Sq	Clambake Charlie Lead	A	RG
493 "B" Sq	Clambake Charlie Hi	A	RG
493 "C" Sq	Clambake Charlie Lo	A	RG

Wg Gnd Sta   Meadowbrook   A
Wg Wx/Mon a/c   Meadowbrook Monitor   A
Div Gnd Sta   Arrowswift   B
Div Collective   Highroad   B
Div Wx a/c(45th)   Zootsuit Purple   B
Div Wx a/c(93rd)   Zootsuit Black   B
Scouting Force:
   Assy A/C   Kodak Control   B
   Route Wx-0600E   Kodak White   B
   Route Wx-0600E to Tgt   Kodak Red   B
Bomber-Fiter:
   Plan "A"   Balance One   C
   Plan "B"   Balance Two   C
Fiter-Bomber:
   Plan "A"   Vinegrove 1-10   C
   Plan "B"   Vinegrove 2-10   C
Fiter Gnd Sect   Colgate   C
Div Authenticator   Cabin
Div Recall Phrase   The sunset Park
Wg Recall Phrase   Hearts and Flowers
Kodak Wx Code: I.P. - 8; Tgt - 9
CARPET: Plan "A" - ON, leaving Eng Cst.
     OFF, leaving enemy territory.
Plan "B" - ON at Belgian Coast
     OFF after crossing enemy lines
     on return.
WINDOW: Plan "A" - 264 units starting at
     I.P. for eleven minutes.
Plan "B" - 264 units starting at I.P.
     for 11 mins. 336 units starting at
     5019 N - 0700 E for 14 mins. (Return)

TIME	FLARE	LETTER
0700-1300	R-RR	L - Love
1300-1900	RG	G - George
1900-0100	Y-YR	Q - Queen

"A&B"   IVERSON - Lt.Col.Fandel
"B"   JONES,J   235 H/X(10) Lt. Bouliane
529 L/D (19)   482 H/A(9)   SAIN
ISAACS   SHERMAN
365 L/S (20)   372 L/K(22)
WERTH   *SCHIFFERER   MOORE   SCHAUS
343 L/I   378 L/K(20)   402 L/P(18)   327 L/R
(19)   *ANDERSON   (20)
     299 L/U (19)
*WAARVICK   WASHBURN
257 L/T (19)   972 L/C(20)

Stations   0635   Taxi   0725
Alert   0645   Code   Tribune
S/Engines   0710   Takeoff   0740
Code   Chicago   Assy.Alt. 18,000 ft.

34 "B" Sq. HIGH

LIVINGSTON - Capt. Simpson
237 H/I(10)
"B"   ABRAMS   RICHARDSON,LS
605 B/H (17)   410 H/J (11)
PEEDE   LERCH
373 B/J(14)   971 B/A (14)
*BUTLER   SPRINGER   *TIGGES   MANN
409 B/H   840 B/E(16)   338 B/M(17)   138 B/I
(15)   THAETE   (15)
     929 H/C (13)
NASS
938 B/C (14)
THOMPSON   BENNETT
331 B/Y (16)   953 B/D(17)

Stations   0635   Taxi   0715
Alert   0645   Code   Examiner
S/Engines   0700   Takeoff   0730
Code   Los Angeles Assy.Alt. 19,000 ft.

34 "C" Sq. LOW

ALLING - Lt. Brown
441 H/S (8)

"B"   DAVIS   FELKER
987 E/F (1)   959 H/R (8)
HENDERSON   MCLEAN
391 E/J(4)   465 E/O (6)
WRIGHT   *O'GRADY   JAMES   MCTAGGAI
403 E/Z(5)   416 E/C(3)   113 E/S(4)   280 E/
ROSCHER   (3)
367 E/L (6)
SHEESLEY   *GIARDINI
263 E/N (7)   266 E/T (2)
STEMEN
309 E/H (6)

Stations   0635   Taxi   0735
Alert   0645   Code   Free Press
S/Engines   0720   Takeoff   0750
Code   Detroit   Assy.Alt. 17,000

GROUND SPARES:
FFF - 358 H/N(11)   G.I.s - 179 E/A (7)
556 H/F(11)   321 B/F (13)
Vis - 991 H/Z (9)   071 B/K (15)
     - Camera A/C   271 L/O (18)

STAND BY CREWS:
Knowlton (18th)   Curtiss (7th)
Wx Monitor A/C: 176 H/Q (6)
Lt. Richardson,Z & Maj. Smith

NOTE: CONTROL TIMES AND FIGHTER
SUPPORT ON REVERSE SIDE.

Handwritten annotations (partial): Target of Opportunity / Bombs fell short but a small residential area was wiped out / Primary Target was Chemnitz / Long mission 8:55 hrs.

Mission plan for February 14, 1945. Writing says: "(Oak Leaf Cluster Mission) Led for Sqd 5 Lead M. New Target of Opportunity. Bombs fell short but small residential area was wiped out.... Primary target was Chemnitz."

the plane while I controlled the air speed and the vertical movement. "I've got the city on my cross hairs!" he yelled into the intercom, nearly drowning out the roar of the engines, and the bombs were released.

"Damn!" Bill yelled a few seconds later. "I see the railroad yards and they're not where they're supposed to be. We missed by a mile! Damn, damn, damn!" We were the lead crew of the high squadron, and every B-17 in the squadron dropped when our bombs were released. Each one of us missed. This was the only time I can recall that Bill missed the target. I think we all suffered for him, sympathizing with his despair that we were hitting civilians and not crippling the city's marshalling yards.

A minute later, a red light came on in the instrument panel. Two five-hundred-pound bombs were hung up in the bomb bay. Bill climbed to the bomb bay walkway—a narrow, tight passage, just over a foot in width. He looked down at the ground twenty-five thousand feet below. He was determined to drop those two bombs. With one quick turn of a wrench, the bombs fell somewhere near Hof.

Instantly, Eddie noticed that Bill was moving his hands in an uncontrolled manner and realized that while Bill was struggling to

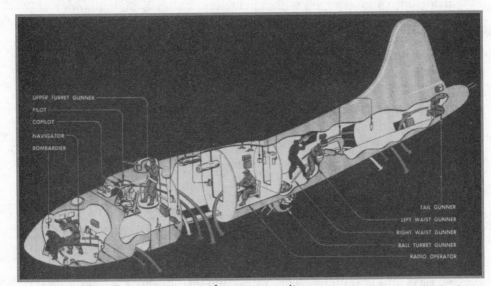

Chart of B-17F crew positions and emergency exits. (*The Comet Connection*. From *A Wing and a Prayer* by Harry H. Crosby. HarperCollins Publishers, 1993.)

release the hung-up bombs he had accidentally pulled the cord loose from his oxygen. With lightening speed, Eddie rushed to the walkway, grabbed Bill with one hand and held on with the other. Eddie made eye contact with him and nodded toward the loose oxygen line. Bill had just enough oxygen left in his brain to understand that he needed to reattach his line to the bottle. Meanwhile, Eddie sensed the unsteadiness of Bill's legs; at any second, they could buckle, and Eddie would not have been able to hold him in the plane. He might have had to let Bill go to keep both of them from falling through. While the oxygen revived Bill, it also gave him the strength to step cautiously into the pilot's compartment and then down the steps into the nose. He turned on the switch that shut the bomb bay door, and sat down with a sigh of relief.

"Pilot to crew," I called on the intercom. "Bill is still with us . . . he's safe."

Bill called to Eddie in the radio room: "I owe you one, Eddie!"

That was another close call.

Later that night, Bill just wanted a hot shower, but it was Tuesday and we were only allowed to shower on Thursday. He didn't want to wait so he walked over to the Women's Army Corps quarters where there were showers. On the way back, he had the misfortune of meeting up with a lieutenant colonel, a commander of one of the squadrons. For some reason, Bill was dressed in a civilian pair of pants and sweater. The lieutenant colonel would not tolerate insubordination, and ordered Bill to stand at attention with his right hand in salute for five minutes. Bill did as he was told, and nearly froze before he returned to the hut. That night it seemed like he shivered for hours as he tried to warm himself by the coal stove in our Nissen hut. Bill wrote a letter to his wife, Nell: "My dearest, when I get home, don't ever let me forget to tell you what happened today, February 14th . . ."

February 20, 1945 The Eighth Air Force continued with some of its heaviest bombing raids. This time, the Eighth and the Royal Air Force joined forces on a raid over Nuremberg, Germany, that lasted two days and two nights. The Americans flew during daylight hours and British Bomber Command flew at night. The raids on

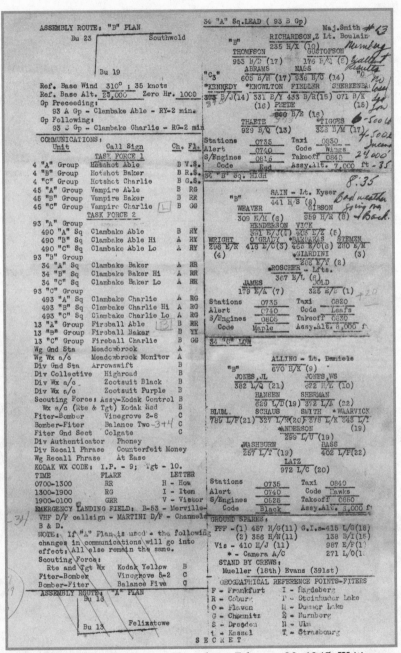

Secret instructions for mission over Nuremberg, February 20, 1945. Writing says: "#13 Nuremberg. Excellent results no losses... Bad weather going over and back."

Nuremberg were intense and devastating, and I recall that we
dropped one-thousand-pound bombs on the city.

In early February, there were raids on Berlin, Hof, Chemnitz, and
Nuremberg, all part of a "big week"—an eight-day bombing blitz by
eleven thousand Allied bombers. The RAF's method was to head
over the target in single file, their route indicated by a pathfinder
plane, and if the weather was clear, the pathfinder dropped flares to
light the target area. Otherwise, the RAF dropped by radar. As for
the big week, press reports described Germany as "reeling under a
merciless hail of high explosives from allied bombers raining down
day and night."[20]

I can only begin to imagine the horror the Germans must have
felt to see hundreds of bombers approaching their city. Ernie Pyle,

*Deadly flak explodes around a formation of B-17s during a mission over Kassel,
Germany.* (USAAF)

the famous war correspondent, wrote this account of witnessing an Eighth Air Force formation en route to a target:

And then a new sound gradually droned into our ears. The sound was deep, and all encompassing, with no notes in it— just a gigantic faraway surge of doom. It was the heavies!

They came from directly behind us, and at first they were mere dots in the sky. You could see clots of them against the far heavens, too tiny to count them individually . . . They came on with terrible slowness . . . in constant procession, and I thought it would never end!

What the Germans must have thought is beyond comprehension. Their march across the sky was slow and steady. I've never known a storm, or a machine, or any resolve of Man, that had about it the aura of such relentlessness. You have the feeling that even if God appeared beseechingly before them in the sky, with palms up to persuade them back, they would not have had within them the power to turn from their irresistible course!

The Germans began to shoot heavy, high ack-ack. Great puffs of it, by the score, spackled the sky until it was hard to distinguish the smoke puffs from the planes.

The formation never varies, but moves on as if nothing had happened. Nothing deviates them! They stalk on slowly, with the dreadful pall of sound, as though they were seeing only something at a great distance and nothing existed in between! [21]

THE STRAGGLER

I saw a Fort knocked out of its group,
Afire and in despair,
With Nazi fighters surrounding her,
As it flew alone back there.

The Messerschmitts came barreling through,
Throwing a hail of lead
At the crippled Fort that wouldn't quit,
Though two of its engines were dead.

But a couple of props kept straining away
And her guns were blazing too
As she stayed in the air in that hell back there
And fought, like Fortresses do.

Four times a fighter belched fire and smoke,
Four times a fighter went down;
As the Fortress kept on winging home
And the nerve of the crew stayed sound.

But time after time the fighters came
And attacked the lagging plane.
I knew she couldn't last for long
And my heart was touched with pain.

Her gunners fought a bitter fight,
But now the guns were still
And a fighter, seeing the time was ripe,
Came in to make the kill.

A stream of lead ripped into a tank
And the Fort exploded in two,
And somewhere the angels prepared a place
For a weary Fortress crew.

—T/Sgt. Orvil (Second Toner) Lindsey

8

Code P: Dresden

——◦◦◦——◦◦◦——

March 2, 1945 At 4:00 A.M. a corporal issued his command: "Gentlemen, rise!" Although I was half asleep and barely able to open my eyes, I saw him standing just inside the door of our hut, his hands clasped behind his back, his feet fast in a rigid stance, precisely nine inches apart, and his shoulders locked.

On this day the lead crews were alerted before dawn. All other crews were allowed to sleep until 5:00 A.M. This extra hour made a difference—anything to delay the inevitable. Lead crews were scheduled to attend a special briefing at 5:30 with the group commander, group navigator, and group bombardier. Rarely were the three leads given a special briefing, so I knew there was something critically important about this mission.

We were told we were flying to Dresden, Germany. This was our ninth mission as lead crew. At the briefing we reviewed the reconnaissance photos which indicated that the city's factories were mass-producing war supplies: shells, rifles, machine guns, V-1 and V-2 rockets. Intelligence had documented shipments of supplies by rail over the bridges of the Elbe River with supply trucks moving over the same arteries to the front seventy-five miles away. Our target in Dresden was the railroad marshalling yard.

The estimated flight time for this mission was ten hours: five hours and fifteen minutes on oxygen, and four hours and forty minutes over enemy territory. Flak was expected en route and over the target, and heavy enemy fighter response was anticipated. As the Germans had fallen back before the Allies in the west and the Russians in the east, the Luftwaffe had become more consolidated and threatening.

By the time the briefing was over, we had memorized the map of Dresden, perhaps permanently. We collected our flak vests, fleece-lined jackets, heated suits, gloves, parachutes, and forty-five-caliber pistols. I grabbed my flight helmet, headset, and throat mike, and threw my oxygen mask over my shoulder along with survival kits with escape routes, candy, and gum. We picked up oranges and Hershey bars on the way out—something I usually did before a flight, though I never recalled taking a bite of anything along the way.

Miss Prudy carried a full load of gas and two tons of general purpose bombs. We did not carry incendiaries. Each plane in the 34th Bomb Group carried fourteen fifty-caliber machine guns, a total of five hundred and forty-six guns in a formation of thirty-nine planes.

At 7:10 A.M. the flare from the control tower signaled time for our departure. As the high squadron lead, we were the second plane in the bomb group to take off. We followed the lead squadron, and the low squadron lead followed us. Once each squadron was assembled, the 34th flew across the English Channel. We knew the identification of the bomb group in front of us as well as the one behind us. A total of eleven bomb groups had assembled over East Anglia, and each group was separated by a two-minute interval.

On March 2, the Eighth Air Force flew raids on three cities. Each had a different code: Magdeburg—code H; Leipzig—code S; and Dresden—Code P. Our method of communication with other lead pilots was simplified with this code. If we were one hundred miles from Dresden, our command pilot would inform the other leads that we were one hundred miles west of P.

Each squadron, group, wing, and division of the Eighth Air Force also had code names assigned for this mission. Our flight plan was taped to the upper leg of my flying suit so I could access these codes quickly. *Miss Prudy*'s code was Heartbeat N Nancy. Our division recall code was "Broadway of America! Broadway of America!" The code for the entire striking force was "High road, High road!" If we were leading the 34th and had to abort the mission, my command pilot would call the two other lead pilots in our group: "This is Heartbeat N Nancy calling High Road, High Road, Broadway of America, Broadway of America!" And then we would start a gradual turn to the right and head back toward England.

The P-51 Mustang fighters, with black and white checkered

FLIGHT PLAN

PILOT _ALLING, C. B._　NAVIGATOR _BASKIN, R. C._　_DRESDEN_　DATE _2 March 1945_

STATIONS	ENGINES	TAXI	T.O. 0620
LEAVE BASE			
COAST OUT		_HWB. 0809_	
ENEMY COAST		_RBA. 25000_	
I.P.		_RBW 30/25_	
TARGET			
ENEMY COAST			

	MORNING TWILIGHT	SUN Rises	Sets	EVENING TWILIGHT	MOON Rises	Sets

WATCH ___ Fast / Slow　RATE ___ secs/hour Gaining / Losing

At ___ G.M.T.

RESTRICTED

FROM / TO	W/V USED	HEIGHT Temp.	I.A.S. MPH /K	T.A.S. (K)	COURSE	DRIFT	TRUE HDNG.	VAR.	MAG. HDNG.	G.S.	DIST.	TIME	E.T.A.	TIME CONTROL POINTS & Rendezvous
BUF 19 / BUF 23	334/37	-11 7000	158	141	012	-6	006	+10	016	118	24	17	0743 07.55	From A2
SOUTHWOLD					087	+0	077	+10	087	149	17	07	08:02	C.P.I ST. CLIMB. 08:08
5244-0438	3/35	-16 11325	159	152	077	-11	066	+9	075	160	96	37	08:45	C.P.I
5229-1820	3/60	-24 18200		172	096	-12	084	+7	091	216	136	38	19:23	
5237-1049	319/88	-31 21900		182	085	-24	061	+5	066	212	91	24	09:47	
5210-1243	317/92	-34 23000		186	111	-9	102	+4	106	268	75	17	10:04	
5139-1254	304/84			168	+20	188	+4	192		232	32	08	10:12	I.P.
5129-1355		-36 23000		184	105	-7	098	+4	102	264	38	09	10:21	TGT.
5105-1405	304/79	-30 21500		181	164	+17	181	+4	185	230	25	06	10:27	R.P.
5021-1358	3/28	-27 21000		177	186	+22	208	+4	212	194	45	12	10:39	
5032-0920					273	+10	283	+5	288	112	178	1:40	12:19	
5008-0805	3/80				243	+24	267	+6	273	132	54	24	12:43	
5005-0700					266	+18	284	+6	290	112	42	23	13:06	C.P.II
5005-0600					270	+17	287	+7	294	110	38	21	13:27	ST. Tower, ALT
5115-0255				172	300					116	49	26	14:27	
SOUTHWOLD					325	+4	329	+7	336	112	81	43	15:12	
BASE					254	+8	262	+10	272	132	22	10	15:22	

FORECAST WINDS		
Alt.		Temp.
Surf.		
5		
10		
15		
20		
25		
30		

FLIGHT RECORD

TIME	COURSE	W/V USED &/OR DRIFT	TRUE HDNG.	MAG. HDNG.	NAVICATIONAL OBSERVATION	GENERAL OBSERVATION	I.A.S. MPH /K	HEIGHT & AIR TEMP	T.A.S.	RUN DIST.	TIME	C.S.	TO RUN DIST.	TIME	E.T.A.
W	Dummer Lake				5139-1254 I.P. for Primary										
H	Hannover				5118-1307 I.P. for Sec.										
1	Magdeburg				5104-1342 TGT.										
S	Leipzig				5021-1358 R.P.										
P	Dresden						5005 0600	C 25	464-1308						

Flight plan of Dresden mission for Miss Prudy _navigator Ray Baskin, March 2, 1945._

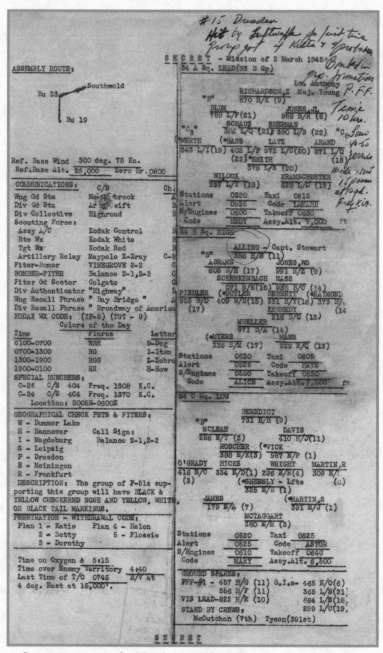

Secret instructions for March 2, 1945, mission over Dresden. (USAAF)

noses and yellow and white or black tail markings, were also given a code for this mission. Our command pilot, Captain Stewart, next to me in the co-pilot's seat, was prepared to call in our Little Friends when bandits approached. Today's code for calling in fighters was "Vinegrove 2-1, 2-2." Our code to call in the fighters was "Vinegrove 2-1" and the code to identify the 34th Bomb Group was "Vinegrove 2-2."

At 8:01 A.M., the 34th assembled, and flew out over Southwold, England, on a sixty-eight degree heading at 10,700 feet.

At 8:33 A.M., Ray asked me to inform the group lead that we were eight miles left of course. The lead changed their heading to eighty degrees and we continued our climb up to sixteen thousand feet.

At 9:39 A.M., we were heading sixty-three degrees northeast and in the distance we could see light flak coming up over the city of Hanover, Germany, just off our left wing.

At 10:09 A.M., we were flying at twenty-four thousand feet. We banked toward a heading of 168 degrees to the Initial Point.

At 10:11 A.M., German fighters appeared suddenly over the horizon, and Captain Stewart made an immediate call to our Little Friends, "Vinegrove 2-1. This is Vinegrove 2-2. Bandits attacking! Bandits attacking! Come in! Over."

One hundred and forty German fighters flew directly toward the bomber stream. Just seconds before impact with the Fortress formations they veered away avoiding a collision. Our bombardier, Bill, taking in the attack through the plexiglass nose, witnessed nine B-17s in the lead group blow up in flames, one after another.

It seemed that the entire Luftwaffe was shooting at us. The Germans attacked the Eighth Air Force with everything they had—Me 109s, Fw 190s, and their sinister-looking new Me 262s. We were on the alert to watch out for the 262s. This two-engine jet had 24mm cannons up front and flew 540 miles per hour. The Me 262 could far outrace our fighters and more than triple the speed of a B-17. It was the fastest plane in the air.

All our guns were blazing and our crew chief, manning the top turret gun three feet above my head, was shooting in a frenzy, his dual fifty-calibers drilling the air like an electric sledgehammer. The noise was deafening. We closed our formation as tightly as I can ever recall so that the guns of all thirty-nine planes in our group could put up a wall of fire against German fighters. If there is a hell, this was

B-17s dropping their bomb loads on a mission over Germany. (USAAF)

it, mixed with strange and unexpected moments of exhilaration in knowing we had strength in unity and numbers.

I had the weird impression of enemy fighters wheeling in the air like hornets. They'd race past and then moments later come ripping again through our formation. In reality, the fighters needed to make large swoops before their next pass. But there were a lot of them in the sky and every time one formation would disappear I'd see another "finger four" from the corner of my eye, closing in against us again, their wings flashing with fire. They came in on us from different directions, and when they appeared in front they closed with incredible speed.

"Bandits at 12 o'clock high!" I yelled into the intercom at one point as a group of Luftwaffe fighters in their peculiar, staggered formation approached us directly head on. All I could do was hold the ship steady and trust in my gunners, and those in the rest of the group, to fend them off. It was like a game of "chicken," their guns blazing while I could hear our own firing back, until the Germans would suddenly fly above us, just seconds from impact.

"Bandits at 6 o'clock!" yelled Glen in the intercom, as another wave of fighters tore at us from behind. We had a thirty-second break, and then more fighters came in.

Next, they flew toward the right side of *Miss Prudy.* "Fighters at 3 o'clock! Look out!" Jack yelled. I wondered how many more attacks we could possibly survive. I couldn't evade, run, or go any faster. I could only hold steady with the group. Moments later another shout came over the intercom. "Bandits at 9 o'clock," yelled Chuck Williams as Me-262s approached the left side of the plane.

As they approached us from either side, they'd take a last second dive under our squadron or soar above, an attack the Luftwaffe orchestrated with precision and a lot of nerve. *Miss Prudy* was by now rattling with return machine-gun fire from all sides. I thought we had a reprieve, at least for a few moments, until I heard Glen yell, "Bandits low and climbing fast!"

Once more, Me 262s suddenly loomed as if from nowhere out of the sky, and as they came at us, they rolled over, shooting at us from all angles. I could see their tracers coming right at us. I was not sure why or how we were still alive, but we kept ploughing through the steady stream of fire. One Me 109 flew so close to our left wing that our waist gunners, Chuck and Jack, could see their bullets hit into the fighter. Jack then turned around and tapped Chuck Williams on the shoulder, pointing down, indicating that another fighter was approaching underneath. Jack let go a steady stream of fire and mortally wounded the German craft. It smoked, flamed, and then the pilot bailed out and his parachute filled. I would still bet that despite the momentary feeling of victory for our gunners, there may have been an unexpected quiet sigh of relief knowing that this man—our enemy—was alive, and that he'd have a second chance at life.

At 10:23 A.M., Ray saw an American ship blow up, no parachutes. Bill saw two P-51s plunge to the earth. Thirty seconds later, we started the bomb run, and Bill managed the steering of the plane, his face glued to his Norden bombsight, guiding *Miss Prudy* to the target.

At 10:27 A.M., Bill yelled, "Bombs away!" and we released our bombs. We were flying at 254 miles per hour ground speed due to heavy tail winds. Our heading was 142 degrees. Our altitude was 24,000 feet. The temperature registered minus thirty-five degrees

A B-17 hit by flak goes down on a bombing mission over Germany. (USAAF)

centigrade. The truth is that Bill had dreaded this moment. He knew that while we were trying to bomb military targets, bombs would also fall on innocent civilians unable to find shelter in a city of six hundred and fifty thousand.

At 10:56 A.M., shortly after we began our return trip, Major Young, the command pilot of the lead squadron, called in, "Heartbeat N Nancy! This is Heartbeat K King! Over."

Captain Stewart replied, masking his concern, "Heartbeat K King! This is Heartbeat N Nancy! Looks like you're in trouble."

"We've lost two engines and have a wounded gunner! Take Over."

"Heartbeat K King. This is Heartbeat N Nancy. Read you loud and clear. Good luck!" Stewart called in with hope and a reassuring voice. Richardson, no longer able to lead the 34th, flew solo in the clouds seeking protection from the German fighters. A fine lead pilot and friend, he was devoted to his crew and determined to get them back to a safe place.

At 11:08 A.M., we assumed the lead position. My high squadron moved into the lead squadron position and the lead group fell back to our initial position.

At 11:58 A.M., the bomb group ahead of us, leading the entire Eighth Air Force, suffered heavy losses. Each of the three lead planes went down one after the next. Just after the last lead was hit, they called in, "We're hit! Take over!"

Their command pilot strained to complete his message as they started their descent. Their planes moved aside in formation as we flew ahead to assume the lead of the Eighth Air Force while the Luftwaffe fired at us. Fortunately, our radar was working and had not yet been jammed. All systems were go. Captain Stewart asked me over the intercom: "Alling, have you ever led the 34th?"

"No, Captain Stewart!"

"Have you ever led the Eighth Air Force before?"

"Hell, no!"

"You're leading both now!" he answered with a command.

I called to Ray over the intercom, "Pilot to navigator. We're now leading the Eighth Air Force. Stay cool, guy. You're the best."

"Got ya!" Ray replied.

Ray Baskin and Mort Narva guided us back from Dresden through corridors of flak. Just moments before landing, I heard Bill's voice on the intercom, "Chuck," he spoke softly, "This is God's honest truth." He paused. "I was scared to death flying over Dresden."

The consolidated, confidential Air Corps lead crew mission report of the Eighth Air Force raid to Dresden on March 2 stated:

Lead Navigator: Baskin, R. (Ray) C, nine lead missions, fighter escort good at rendezvous. Enemy aircraft were reported to be attacking from the rear of bomber stream. Majority of fighter escort left to meet this attack. Main enemy aircraft formation then attacked rear of column. Lead radar navigator, M. (Mort) I. Narva. Target picked up at forty miles. Scope drift method not used. Course to target was seven miles east of I.P. Bombing was done in group formation and all squadrons dropped on the lead. Radar navigator in this squadron called rate checks from eleven to eighteen miles—last one good. Thinks bombs landed in center of town. The lead aircraft of the high squadron took over the lead of the group about fifteen minutes after bombs away and lead squadron moved aside. The Lead is reported to have landed on the continent but no more information is available.[22]

Eleven hundred and fifty-nine B-17s and B-24s in the 1st, 2nd, and 3rd Divisions of the Eighth Air Force flew over Magdeburg, Dresden, and Chemnitz that day. The Eighth was escorted back by six hundred and seventy-five fighters.[23]

Four hundred and eight American planes bombed Dresden. During the raid, sixty-seven German planes were reported severely damaged. The 34th destroyed six fighters and severely damaged four. The Eighth Air Force lost nineteen bombers.

Captain Richardson's crippled plane flew back across Germany dodging into every piece of cloud cover it could find. It just barely made it to Luxembourg, where Richardson and his crew were interned until the end of the war. Just days after the Dresden raid, we learned that his gunner, John Frey, had died on board the flight before they were able to land and get help. John was a buddy of the enlisted men in my crew, and he was always with our guys on the base. His death weighed heavily on them and for weeks afterward, I could sense their painful sadness—the heavy sorrow when a friend dies in combat.

I'll never forget the sight of Richardson's slow descent into the clouds, smoke trailing from his wing. We couldn't keep track of him. I hated to think of him flying alone in that fighter-infested sky without the support of our Little Friends. I never knew what had happened to Richardson until the end of the war when I learned that thankfully he and the rest of his crew had survived.

Dresden was the epicenter of a combined assault by the British and the Americans. As for the British, Churchill's contempt for Germany ran deep. After the Battle of Britain (August 15 to September 15, 1940), Air Marshal Hermann Goering had switched from daylight bombing operations to night raids over London. With each raid, during the Blitz, he sent two hundred or more planes nightly from September 1940 until May 1941, weather permitting. The Germans dropped explosives and incendiaries on the nerve center of London and entire rows of houses were hit just as badly. The outlook at this time, which Churchill admitted, was that London, except for some of its strong buildings, would be gradually reduced to a heap of rubble. The raids on London killed 40,000 and left 375,000 homeless.[24]

Other cities, including Coventry, Bristol, Birmingham, and Southhampton were also fire bombed and terrorized. While history may recount these events differently, it was suspected that in bombing Dresden, the British wanted to retaliate for the German bombing of heavily populated cities in England.

The March 2nd raid over Dresden was not the first. The city was bombed by the Royal Air Force on the night of February 13 and into the early morning hours of the 14th. The Eighth Air Force then bombed Dresden on the morning of the 14th. The RAF returned to Dresden during the night of March 1, and knocked out what was left of the air-raid alarms. Smoke from the intense fires from the RAF bombing was still raging throughout the city, and by the time we flew over Dresden, the fires nearly obscured our target area.

It is difficult to find reliable figures of the casualties in Dresden, although it is estimated that more than thirty-five thousand perished on March 1 and 2. (Far more had died in the February raids.) The damage done was too horrifying to contemplate. Years later, the Americans learned that thousands of people had been fleeing the Russians's advance and happened to be in Dresden at the time of the raids.

Sadly, Dresden was torched. The once beautiful city was consumed with fires generated by exploding bombs, reaching a temperature of three thousand degrees Fahrenheit on the ground; enough heat to melt a stone wall. The glorious Frauenkirche Cathedral (Church Of Our Lady) was destroyed as well—although the cathedral never took a direct hit, it could not withstand the heat and reverberations from the bombs.

Two days later, the Germans retaliated, and seventy Junker 288s flew into East Anglia, and circled our field, even though all our lights were out. One plane spotted a truck driving up the main road with its lights on—against all the regulations. The truck was strafed. Days later, we heard that Hitler ordered the head of the German Luftwaffe, Herman Goering, to execute all British and American airmen in the POW camps in Germany because of the March 2 raid over Dresden. Goering refused to carry out the order.

———•◦•—◦◦—•◦•———

Fifty-four years later, on July 7, 1999, *The York County Coast Star* newspaper which covers southern Maine, published the following article written by Peter Huchthausen, a good friend, author, and a man with impressive credentials. He is a former navy captain, commanding officer of a river boat division in the Vietnam War, and Naval attaché to Moscow.

COLLATERAL DAMAGE

I can never sleep on the flight from Boston to London, and this time lost myself in conversation with a sympathetic German couple sitting in the row with me. The lady was attractive, and displayed an obvious love for the English language. Whenever I put my best German forward she countered in exquisite English. She was originally from Dresden, born after the war. She related to me how her father, a Wehrmacht officer serving in the Sixth Army of the famed General Paulus, had been captured and spent five years as POW in Stalingrad. He was happily one of few who came home. He returned to his home in Dresden in 1950 to find his wife and two children had died during the . . . air raids on March 1-2, 1945.

I listened intently to the lady's account of her family, knowing there was a connection here. A friend of mine in Kennebunk had flown in the raid on March 2 against Dresden. That day Charles Alling was a young first lieutenant pilot of the lead B-17 of the High Squadron in the Third Division of the 34th Bomber Group, Eighth U.S. Air Force, flying out of Mendlesham County Norfolk, England. Charles is an unassuming man, yet one you would want on your side in a fight.

On this mission the lead aircraft... [of the group] lost two engines in heavy flak as they ... [came off] their primary target—the rail and transportation center [of] Dresden and that city's industrial munitions complex. The Red Army was 70 miles east and driving rapidly toward the city. British raids by 1,400 bombers had struck Dresden the night before.

With the lead aircraft badly hit and dropping out of formation, one gunner dead and two engines gone, Chuck Alling slid his aircraft into the vacant position and automatically assumed lead and took them . . . [away from] Dresden. The rest is history, from 36,000 to 60,000 citizens were lost, depending on whose figures you cite.

After hearing the lady's story of her father, and the loss of what would have been her stepmother and half brother and sister, I told her about Chuck Alling, and how after completing his required missions, and receiving the Distinguished Flying Cross and the Air Medal with four Oak Leaf Clusters, he returned home, graduated from Yale in 1947, and eventually became a senior partner of SpencerStuart, an international executive recruiting firm. In 1988, Alling studied ethics in Oxford University Graduate School, and was co-founder and . . . chairman of the Foundation for Leadership, Quality, and Ethics in New York City. He was recently appointed by the Secretary of Defense to the Air Force University Board of Visitors at Maxwell Air Force Base in Montgomery, Alabama.

After describing what sort of man Chuck Alling was, I noticed the German lady seemed moved and leaned forward suddenly and showed me her watch. Emblazoned on the face next to an embedded chip of stone rubble, was a silhouette in black of the famed Dresden Cathedral of Our Lady, one of the most beautiful edifices in Germany, destroyed during the raids of March 1945. Superimposed in gray on the back was the silhouette of the ruined cathedral, as it had been maintained by the East German authorities for 50 years as a monument to the lost. After German reunification in 1990, residents of Dresden began the long and painful reconstruction of the cathedral and raised funds partially through the sales of these wrist watches.

At that moment, the German lady and I simultaneously

came to the same conclusion. Chuck Alling had to have one. She took off her watch and gave it to me saying, "Please give this to your friend as an act of friendship." With the image of that conversation at 30,000 feet above the Atlantic searing into my mind, I watched the lush green fields of England flicker below us just as they had beneath Alling's bomber as it climbed out on his mission that day in 1945.

I saw the German couple again at a distance after going through British customs at Heathrow, and I noted a sort of glow surrounding the lady. She smiled, her eyes sparkling with a kind of excitement at sharing our secret plan.

Some weeks later I presented it to Chuck after a service at St. David's Church in Kennebunk. Chuck was surprised and moved. I told him the facts as related to me by the smiling lady from Germany, of how, when the reconstruction work first began on the cathedral, engineers discovered that not a single high explosive bomb had hit the edifice directly, and that the roof had probably caught fire from the incendiary bombs which had ignited adjacent buildings, causing the cathedral finally to collapse.[25]

I wear the wristwatch as a reminder of Iris Riechel and her kind gesture. I wrote to thank her for the watch, and asked for her forgiveness for the final American bombing over Dresden.

Several weeks later, Peter Huchthausen was in Berlin overseeing the filming of his book. He called on Iris who was living in Bovenden, Germany, with her husband, two sons, and a daughter. She was surprised and delighted to hear from Peter and invited him down for the weekend. Peter arrived on a Friday evening and spent a few nights with the Riechels. There she told Peter that she had given me the watch to ask for forgiveness for what the Germans had done during the war.

On Saturday morning, their daughter, in her late teens, left the house for a long walk. On Sunday morning, just as she was about to leave again, Peter inquired as to where she was headed. "If you would like to come with me, I will show you," she replied.

The two walked a long path up the side of a steep hill. Once they arrived at the top, Peter saw they had reached a graveyard, nestled in a grove of trees—a Jewish gravesite with the Star of David on each stone. The young woman went about her self-appointed chore of cleaning the stones. When she tired, they left and walked silently, in deep thought, down the steep hillside path back to her home.

This moment of solitude and reflection, in its perfect and absolute simplicity, reveals much about an individual and family whose acts of kindness and forgiveness on behalf of their country become all the more poignant. The marred past must not be forgotten, and even the hideous memories must stay alive. This family's gesture, and others like it, may help a nation begin to heal.

DAWN

The immortal spirit hath no bars
To circumscribe its dwelling place;
My soul hath pastured with the stars
Upon the meadow lands of space.

My mind and ears at times have caught
From realms beyond our mortal reach,
The utterance of eternal thought
Of which all nature is the speech.

And high above the seas and lands
On peaks just tipped with morning light,
My dauntless spirit mutely stands
With eagle wings outspread for flight.

—Frederick George Scott[26]

9

Now the Day Is Over

━━•◆•━━

March 15, 1945   Our nineteenth mission was to Oranienburg, Germany, twenty miles north of Berlin. Our target—
the marshalling yards. Reconnaissance photos indicated
that freight cars were packed with shipments of war supplies, and
Intelligence believed those supplies would be used to defend the capital. Our departure for Oranienburg was like so many others. We
flew from Mendlesham in thick fog and light rain. Ray recalled those
moments:

> We couldn't see the end of the runway. I lost sight of the plane
> ahead; regardless, B-17s continued to take off exactly thirty
> seconds after the plane ahead started to roll. It was just day-
> light and we started to move ahead in the dense fog and driz-
> zle. We were carrying a full load of fuel and two and a half
> tons of bombs.
>
> About three quarters of the way down the runway and
> shortly after our tail wheel lifted, someone shouted into the
> intercom, "Look out!" I looked up and saw a blinking tail light
> dead ahead. We were closing in on the plane in front of us.
> Chuck saw it, too, and to avoid a runway collision, he yanked
> back on the wheel, forcing *Miss Prudy* to suddenly lift herself
> off the runway. She groaned as she gained altitude long before
> she had the momentum to do so. It was several seconds before
> I was sure *Miss Prudy* could remain flying without stalling out
> and falling to the earth. Somehow Chuck was able to get the

nose down, just enough for the airspeed to build up and the plane to settle down to normal performance. I heard Chuck Williams down below in the ball turret yell, "My God! He nearly wiped my butt with his rudder!"

It seemed miraculous that *Miss Prudy* lifted herself up and over a nineteen and a half foot tail of the B-17 dead ahead. A second later and both ships would have blown up upon impact, our nose against their tail and then several tons of bombs and ammo merging into one great explosion. We never should have made it. A B-17 requires a gradual ascent once she is ready to leave the ground. If the fortress lifts off the ground too early, she will stall and crash. That is one reason the takeoff is a critical maneuver. There were hundreds of casualties during the war of planes that never made it past the end of the runway. This was one of our many close calls. I don't understand why or how we made it through, except I have to

A sample of a map from the briefing room of Mendlesham air base showing the I.P., target, and rally point for the 34th Bomb Group. (USAAF)

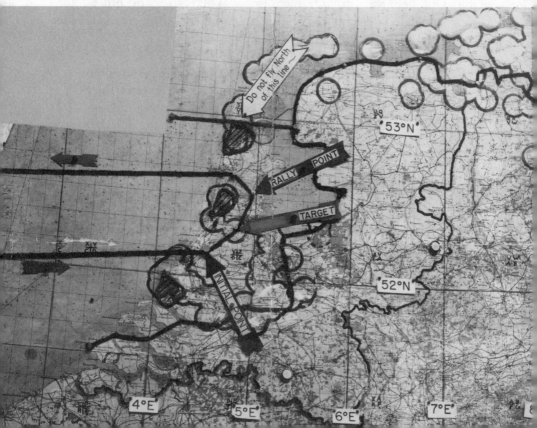

think we were watched over and protected. We could never have done it by ourselves.

Once we had assembled into formation, we settled down on our route to the target. The weather on the approach to Germany was clear for a change: a bombardier's dream. The bomb run was smooth, and with good visibility we knew we hit the target. By the time we returned to Mendlesham, the photos had been developed, and we were informed the air strike was a success; the marshalling yards were crippled. Bill's bomb rating for the day—"very good." (The Air Corps did not hand out a better rating).

On the return flight, I slipped into a reverie, humming a hymn to myself: "*Now the day is over, Night is drawing nigh, Shadows of the evening, Steal across the sky . . .*" I have been told that I do not sing on tune, but that shouldn't really matter; besides, singing and humming is a personal experience. What mattered is that hymns always gave me strength. Unbeknownst to me, though, I had pressed my thumb on the intercom button, allowing my crew to listen in. I was told that I slid around notes, into notes, up and over running notes, half notes and whole notes. I missed the tone and moved from one key to the next. I was horrified to realize that everyone was listening.

Bill stepped in to make light of things and help ease my embarrassment. "It's okay, Chuck, you're just like a hummingbird." I couldn't imagine where he was going with this, and he continued. "Do you know why hummingbirds can't sing? They can't keep a tune!"

Later, in the mess hall, Bill and I talked about the incident on the runway. We learned that the plane in front of us had lost an engine and was incapable of taking off. He was not able to report into the control tower because he was on radio silence—all planes were on radio silence as they left on a mission. Still, he failed to taxi off the runway onto the grass to stay clear of other planes. At dinner I got hold of the pilot, letting him know that his lousy judgment had put all of our lives in danger.

That night, I couldn't get to sleep. Stirring the coals, I sat down alone. I looked into the fire and the flames warmed my soul. Completely absorbed in thought, reflecting on that morning's departure, I couldn't shake the sight of that Fortress suddenly breaking through the fog. I had known *Miss Prudy* was barely ready to take

off and we couldn't possibly turn right or left since we were traveling at 140 miles an hour.

I kept thinking about Prudy and wondering what she would be
doing if she were still alive. I tried to sense her presence, but I could-
n't. Reaching down in my footlocker, I pulled out her handwritten
copy of the 23rd Psalm. Although I knew each word, I still read each
one carefully, as if she had just written them down. And I thought of
what she said to me during my last visit home before she died. I
could remember everything so clearly. "If you are to fly overseas and
I do not have a chance to see you again, I want to say goodbye now
and give you something to hold on to. I want you to take this psalm
and carry it with you always. When you feel worried, frightened or
anxious, hold onto this, and remember that I always love you and
that I'm always with you." Clutching the crinkled paper, I fell asleep.
The next morning, I woke up feeling rested. When I stepped out of
bed, the paper with the psalm fell to the floor. I picked it up, and
placed it back in my breast pocket, and carried it with me through
another day.

The following day, we were granted a three-day pass. Everyone
needed a break. I put on my new Eisenhower jacket, with its tightly
fitted waist and side buckles, threw a small satchel of clothes over
my shoulder and left alone for London and Oxford.

Arriving in London, I walked to the Red Cross Club, booked a
room and slept soundly for fourteen hours. The next morning, I took
a long hot bath and ate a hearty breakfast. At the railroad station I
bought a train ticket for Oxford, seventy-five miles to the west. In
Oxford, I walked up High Street in the heart of the city, dropped my
bag at a Red Cross Club, and left for a warm ale and sandwich in a
local tea room. There were lots of guys like me with a bit of time on
their hands. Some came to read the newspaper but the tea room was
alive with conversation and ideas. It was almost surreal; just a few hundred miles away, the German war machine was weakening at the knees.

I realized the tea room was crowded and people were queuing
up. Among them was an attractive young woman with a friendly
face. I got up from the table, went over to her and said, "It's kind of
crowded here and a long wait, would you like to join me?"

"Delighted," she said and followed me to my table when the maitre d' stopped us. "This lady has to wait her turn in line." I put my arm around her and said, "She's my sister." I knew he didn't believe me and he shouldn't have. I pulled a chair out for her. She sat down and with a smile, she said, "Well, Yank." I apologized for being so forward and explained, "I just wanted you to join me."

That was Dora Miles. She was studying to be a nurse. Her family lived in London and she was visiting her uncle in Stanton Harcourt just outside of Oxford. My uniform said everything about my vocation. Dora asked me where I was staying. I told her and she asked, "Why not come out to our house for dinner? My uncle would love to meet you. Just take the number 18 bus which makes one stop in our village and we're only a two or three minute walk. You can't possibly miss it. My uncle's home is number 322. It has a thatched roof and good plumbing and electricity." That seemed fine, particularly the plumbing. "Six o'clock," she said as we parted. I told her that I would be there and I meant it. I knew I had to arrive precisely at the appointed hour. (Guests in England have been known to take an extra loop around the block, biding time just to arrive at the precise minute.)

In the afternoon, I walked all over Oxford, through lovely courtyards and colleges, visiting the Bodleian Library, the centerpiece of Oxford, and the Christopher Wren Octagonal Theater across the street. It was soon time to catch the bus which, of course, was right on schedule. I stepped off the bus and walked along the cobblestone street in search of the thatched roof, a difficult task as nearly every roof was thatched. It was all quaint—cottages were snug and close together with gardens lovingly cared for. I found number 322, and realized that I was one minute early. With time to spare, I walked in a slow, awkward circle in front of the house, painfully aware of each step as if I had just learned where to place my feet. At precisely six o'clock, I tapped on the door with the cast-iron knocker. Dora answered. She was dressed in a simple starched, ironed frock, and she was radiant. She led me into the living room, a warm room with low ceilings. I met her Uncle Harry seated in his favorite chair next to the fireplace.

Dora poured two glasses of sherry. Harry was already ahead of us. The conversation quickly focused on Harry, a World War I pilot, and he was delighted with that. While Harry was captivated by his own stories, I was captivated with Dora and the delicious meal. It became clear, however, that Harry had become a permanent fixture in our conversation so I asked Dora if she would like to go to a pub in Oxford. She gave me an understanding and appreciative look in return. Harry had an extra gas ration coupon, and offered to drive us in. Dora declined graciously, and we departed with the gas coupon in hand.

The pub was active and packed with flyboys—American airmen from nearby airdomes. We staked out our own space, standing room only, and ordered two ales. Finally, I was able to concentrate on Dora, looking into her lovely dark eyes, full of expression and warmth. She didn't wear makeup, unlike other women with heavy red lipstick and layers of rouge that required a chisel to remove. Her natural looks made her all the more refreshing. Our conversation was wonderful—there was no doubt that she would be fun to get to know. Before long the crowd in the pub thinned out. I just wanted to be alone with her and hold her. Her mouth was soft and alive. What we wanted would not happen that night. We'd have to wait. I was torn inside. I had one day left on my leave and I had promised to meet the crew the following day in Felixstowe. That was my commitment and I hoped that Dora understood. She wrote down her phone number, "Please call," she said. We said goodbye and I stood there on the empty street, waved to her, and watched her drive back to Stanton Harcourt.

I walked slowly back to the Red Cross Club where it was nice to have my own room for a change, but I couldn't get to sleep. "Hey big guy," I thought, "You still have a war to fight. There are guys on the ground in Germany ready to blow you out of the sky with 88mm cannons aimed at your gut. It's you or them. And there are smart German pilots ready to shoot tracers directly at you. You can't let your guard down now. You can't afford to daydream about Dora or any woman for a second. You've got to keep a cool head. It's been sharp and clear so far, and it's worked. Besides, you've got nine other men in your plane depending on you, and they want to see this through." I decided that I'd wait to call Dora until the war was over.

The next morning, I left for Felixstowe, ten miles east of Ipswich on the English Channel. This was the first time our entire crew had taken time off together—officers and non-commissioned officers. It was a memorable moment for all of us. Willie Green, Chuck

Williams, Jack Brame, and Eddie Edwards had just made tech sergeant. (There was only one enlisted rank higher—master sergeant—and that was generally reserved for permanent army personnel). I looked around at my guys with appreciation. They were the best at their job. We were devoted to each other. This was our kind of camaraderie, and it worked for us.

———— •✦• •✦• ————

March 23, 1945   We were scheduled to fly to Giesecke, a small town just south of Dortmund in western Germany. Our target—the railroad yards. In the briefing, we were told to expect light flak over the target area.

The weather was unusually mild and clear with ground visibility and light winds at altitude. After the bomb run, we headed south and crossed the Rhine to avoid flak in the Ruhr industrial area. I asked Bill how accurate we were in hitting the target. "Well," he said, "It's like the time the cow jumped over the fence—udderly ruined." I imagined the Air Corps would agree, except they would say "good."

On our return flight, we took a slight turn to the west when I saw a few bursts of flak in the distance. Ray recalled our position at that moment:

> I just recorded our flying position—50° 43' N, 07° 47' E—26 miles west of Bonn—Time: 13:45z altitude 19,500 ft—when off my right side, I noticed a solo B-17 sliding over toward us to join in our formation. I moved to the right side of the nose as far as my mike cord and oxygen hose would permit, crawling on my knees. I had a good view of him and the bursts of flak around us. I watched him guide his plane over toward our squadron until he flew in formation off the right wing of our deputy lead.

Ray called my attention to this bomber. I thought the pilot must have lost his group and needed to fly with us so the Germans would have less chance to pick him off. My command pilot and I were not terribly concerned until I tried to reach him on the radio and there was no response. We thought perhaps his radio was busted and therefore he was not able to identify himself or his group. We didn't feel there was anything particularly unusual about this. In fact, it seemed understandable, although unexpected.

We continued flying, and I stayed in communication with my deputy lead. He was flying in perfect formation, wingtip to wingtip. My command pilot thought he was a fine pilot, "Alling, keep your eye on your deputy. He's next in line for lead pilot."

"I know him. He'll make a fine lead pilot," I responded full of conviction, "He'll be one of the best."

I looked over at my deputy, and I hoped he would soon join the ranks of lead pilots. He gave me a thumbs up. Things were going well, all systems go as we returned to England. I looked back at my instruments to take a quick read, and then, out of the corner of my eye, I saw a flash. I thought this was just another menacing explosion of flak. Ray yelled, "No!" I looked to my right, expecting to see flak, and there was nothing. To my horror, my deputy's plane was gone.

"Check for parachutes!" I yelled even though there was absolutely nothing anyone could do. That was a useless command. Another fine pilot and crew of young men had been blown out of the sky. Ray described what happened: "The solo B-17 was flying in perfect formation with us, slightly above our wingman. Suddenly, a burst of flak hit his left wingtip and tore it off. His plane made a sudden descent onto the mid-section of our right wingman's plane splitting it in two. The solo B-17 exploded. Our right wingman's plane broke apart: the forward half plunged straight down while the rear section of the plane spiraled to the earth."

Having held so much hope for my deputy who, like many, had so much potential, I felt a terrible sadness for the ten young men on board that plane. There was absolutely nothing we could do for them, but it has gnawed away at me.

All of us then understood that a German had been flying a captured B-17, and when he joined our formation he was able to report our altitude and speed to the German antiaircraft gunners below, giving them the opportunity to direct shells to explode at our exact altitude. The German pilot surely hadn't expected to be hit himself, but he gave his life while we lost many.

March 30, 1945   We were briefed for Hamburg, Germany, the country's second largest city, noted for its seaport, its complex of submarine pens and large synthetic oil refineries. Hamburg had been hit repeatedly by both Bomber Command and the Eighth Air Force, but was still functioning, to a degree, as a haven for warships, prompting Eighth Air Force headquarters to launch a massive air strike.

As we flew over Hamburg, the flak was worse than we had ever seen, particularly as land batteries were supplemented by guns from warships in the harbor. The Germans never let up and every plane in our group was hit by flak. And then the Luftwaffe pounced on us. A B-17 in our squadron was severely damaged and two crew members badly wounded.

Periodically I'd have moments of doubt and this was one. I wondered if we would return today. I am sure others felt that way. How could we not? But we had to keep going. As we flew toward the Channel, with our Little Friends protecting us above, I started to fade and lose track of everything. Losing consciousness, my head fell forward onto the steering wheel. My command pilot, looking out his right window at the incoming Luftwaffe fighters, did not notice what had happened until *Miss Prudy* started to bank slightly to the right. He grabbed the wheel with his right hand and with his other hand yanked on Willie Green's leg. Willie was standing in the top turret above us, firing at the German fighters and didn't appreciate the tug on his leg, until he heard the command pilot yell at a decibel louder than the roar of the engines, exploding shells, and machine gun bullets: "Alling's lost his oxygen!" Willie jumped from his perch, grabbed the emergency oxygen mask, yanked my head back from the steering wheel and held the mask tightly against my face until I regained consciousness. That's when I realized that my oxygen cord had been severed by flak and it was dangling from my headpiece.

In the meantime, our squadron formation had come loose and the Germans fighters threatened to pick us off, one by one. My command pilot resumed speed and altitude and we returned to the lead position, the other ships tightening up behind us. I don't know how long I was out; I just felt hazy for a few moments when I came around. Looking over at my command pilot with appreciation I smiled, "You saved my life."

During the remainder of the trip, all was quiet until we arrived over England and Bill interrupted our silence. "I just saw a doe leaping out of the woods." We braced ourselves for another one of his

Willie Green in the turret of Miss Prudy. (USAAF)

antics. "I bet I know what she's thinking," he continued. "'That's the last time I'll do that for two bucks!'"

Thank God for Bill's whimsical humor, his effervescent spirit, and his gentle way with all of us. We landed, I shut off the engines, and Willie and I walked together from the plane. "Willie," I said, as I wrapped my arm tightly around his shoulder, "You guys saved my life. I owe you everything I've got!"

"That's not much!" he yelled loudly above the roar of the engines, his face bursting into a broad grin.

"I don't care! You saved my life!" I yelled back. Our voices were drowned by the noise around us, but not our spirits. Nothing could take that away.

It was Good Friday. At 6:00 P.M., Bill and I went to the base chapel. I cupped my face with my hands in a moment of silence and thanks, my eyes filling with tears. We whispered our prayers. I prayed for my crew and for my family. I am sure Bill prayed that he'd see his wife sooner rather than later.

Bill, Ray, and I went to the Officers' Club that night. Guys were talking about casualties at the base. During the month of March, the 34th had lost three B-17s in mid-air collisions during group assembly in heavy cloud cover. That was a sobering thought. More than once, I had avoided that same catastrophe by a hair. I knew we were fortunate—luck, so far, was holding with us.

That night Lieutenant Colonel William J. Hershenow Jr., our 4th Squadron commander, approached our table at the club. He put his arm on my shoulder and handed me two pairs of captain's bars. "Congratulations, Captain Alling!" he said enthusiastically.

"Thank you, Colonel Hershenow!" I replied, holding back an overwhelming sense of joy and pride in my crew.

Bill knew it was up to him to come up with some fun in what could otherwise digress into an emotional evening. "You know, Chuck is so excited about his new bars that you watch, he'll wear them on his pajamas tonight."

I quickly reminded Bill that neither I nor any airman had the luxury of owning pajamas. "Bill," I replied, "how could I possibly buy pajamas? I don't have any doe, not even two bucks!"

On June 22, 1945, Drew Middleton, correspondent for *The New York Times*, covered the Allied raids over Hamburg that decimated the city:

Those who fear the revival of German militarism should see Hamburg. The greatest of north German ports lies shattered, burned and empty.

Here are the simple facts of what Allied air power did to Hamburg.

According to a German police estimate made before the city was captured by the British, Allied bombs had killed about 400,000 persons of a pre-war population of 1,682,000.

About 80 percent of the buildings are damaged and approximately 60 percent have been destroyed, according to estimates made by experts of the Eighth Air Force and Bomber Command of the Royal Air Force.

Refineries and port ruined. The oil refineries and port facilities that made Hamburg great are wrecked. Rhenania Ossag Mineralolwerke, Ebans Asphalt and Mineralol Werke and Thorls Vereinigte Harburgen Olfabriken Werke, all natural oil refineries located on small peninsulas jutting into the Elbe, have been so badly damaged by bombs of the Eighth Air Force that the Germans admit their repair is impossible within three years.

The port area was hit with 6,938 tons of American bombs and the British bomb tonnage in the same area was half again as high. One of the largest cranes in the world stands twisted and torn. Its silhouette looks like the skeleton of some prehistoric monster.

The black waters of the port are rimmed with the hulks of sunken ships. Seven of the eight large drydocks of the Blohm and Voss shipbuilding yards have been sunk. Broken hulls of submarines lie in the ways, while in the assembly areas stand huge round slices of prefabricated submarines like sections of gigantic fish.[27]

On Easter Sunday, I left for the evening service. In muted tones, we sang a hymn: *"The strife is o'er, The battle done, The victory of life is won, The song of triumph has begun . . ."* Ever since, this hymn has churned me up inside; not when I hear my voice, of course, but when I consider the words, which resonate like no other.

While I can't remember the rest of the service, I do recall a private epiphany as I sat in the wooden pew. That's when I realized that part of the war experience was my own battle to find a sense of peace while surrounded by chaos. Once I accepted all that existed, without being fatalistic, I felt new resolve, and that acceptance gave me the strength to go on.

I suspect that some of my crew may have felt the same way, but we kept our thoughts to ourselves so I never knew. And it didn't really matter. What mattered is that we were stronger today than yesterday, and I sensed we felt prepared for our final missions in the war, and whatever was to follow.

CARRY ON!

They have not fought in vain, our dead
Who sleep amid the poppies red:
Their plea, attested with their blood,
By all the world is understood.

They fought for peace, as now do we;
Their conflict was for liberty,
For freedom from the blight of war –
And is that still worth fighting for?

We strive no longer men in arms;
We fight not, stirred by war's alarms:
We vow to seal our broken past
With fellowship and friendship fast.

By those who faced the battling years
Let earth forget her warlike fears,
That Freedom, idol of our sires,
May pledge to all her sacred fires.

—Thomas Curtis Clark[28]

10

Music of Angels

————•◆•————

By April 1945, the interior of Germany was bending under the weight of Allied air power which had destroyed its industrial base, fuel resources, and transportation network. At the same time, the vaunted Wehrmacht was falling back on all fronts. The great industrial valley of the Ruhr had been surrounded by Allied ground troops. The Allied armies in the west stretched across the Rhine, while the Soviet armies in the east were streaming across the flatlands of Poland toward Berlin. Soon, German territory would be overrun by the Allies and the Russians. Intelligence had every reason to expect that Hitler would capitulate by June 1.

April 14, 1945   We were briefed for an air strike over Royan, France. This was our twenty-fifth mission and our first group lead. Colonel Creer entrusted us with his entire beloved 34th Bomb Group. I sat in the briefing room and listened to our instructions, never flinching, though I felt the tension of the moment. More than thirty other crews were willing to follow the *Miss Prudy* over enemy territory. They had confidence in us and I knew they would keep in tight formation behind their lead and give us everything they had. And if we fell, they would step in.

The briefing officer described our mission, "Royan is along the coast of France where a fortress guards the port of Bordeaux . . ." It was known that the long guns at Royan had continually harassed Allied shipping and planes returning from Germany. The officer continued, "Flak should be light over the target."

Captain Charles Alling at the controls of his B-17 Miss Prudy. (USAAF)

As we sat at the end of the runway, waiting for the signal from the tower, I looked out my window and there were thirty-eight bombers with engines whirring, waiting to follow. Each ship was prepared to drop nearly three tons of high explosives on the target. The power unleashed by only one Flying Fortress was difficult to comprehend. If the group dropped as planned, the enemy guns would be obliterated.

Since our assignment called for great precision, we flew over the target at fifteen thousand feet—low for us. The official results: Lead Squadron and High Squadron of the 34th, "good." Low Squadron, "poor." But the guns at Royan were forever silenced, and their batteries would never touch an Allied sailor or airman again.

After we landed back at Mendlesham, I quickly cut off the engines and jumped down from the escape hatch. Colonel Creer stepped out of his olive-colored command car and we met halfway. He gave me a hearty handshake, and I introduced him to each member of the crew. He addressed Bill, our bombardier: "The strike photos have been developed. Your results are good." Creer put his arm around my shoulder, and said, "Come on, Alling, I'll give you a ride to the debriefing session."

April 17, 1945   Our next task was to traverse the entire Third Reich in a mission designed to support the Soviet army attacking from the east. "Roudnice, Czechoslovakia," said the briefing officer, "a transportation hub on the eastern front standing in the way of the Russian advance. Your gas tanks have been topped off for a ten-hour trip. Target weather should be clear. Little flak, if any, is anticipated at the target, and fighter opposition is not expected."

Before we left the briefing block, we were given a small piece of cloth, the size of a large handkerchief, with an imprint of the American flag and the Russian phrase, "Ya Amerikanets!" (I'm an American). We were told to carry this cloth in the left breast pocket of our flying suit. If we had to parachute and were spotted by Russian troops, we were to raise our hands, holding the cloth and call out, "Ya Amerikanets!"

Ray followed the assigned route to avoid flak batteries. So far, so good, and Bill steered the *Miss Prudy* on the bomb run over the target. "Bombs away!" he yelled. There was a long pause as the bombs sailed through the sky, and then I heard Bill shout exultantly, "We hit it! Bulls-eye!"

I turned to the command pilot and gave him a thumbs up. He nodded, feigning a smile with a slight look of approval. He was not known for his friendly disposition or overt enthusiasm. Ray gave me the return heading. I checked all the instruments and power settings, looked at my watch, and calculated that as we were heading into the west wind, it would take us five hours to return to the base.

An hour into our return trip, I spotted bursts of antiaircraft shells dead ahead—possibly twenty miles away—at precisely our altitude. My immediate reaction was to steer the group around the flak and then get back on course. Suspecting the flak was localized, coming from guns mounted on flatbed railroad cars, I said to the command pilot, "I'm going to make a slow bank to the left to avoid trouble ahead." I felt a tremendous responsibility not only for my crew, but for the thirty-eight planes behind me.

He signaled with both hands to continue straight ahead. "We don't know if there are German fighters in the area!" His voice was strident with authority.

"Major," I pleaded, "we are very close to the Allied lines. We're heading toward the flak, and if we veer away, our Little Friends will stay with us." We continued arguing for a moment. Neither one of us would give in. I could not let a stream of planes fly for no reason through a wall of flak. He was becoming increasingly agitated, and I counted each second as we closed in on the curtain of antiaircraft fire.

"Major, I think it's best that we alter our course. We can't chance it!" I didn't give him time to respond and took immediate action, banking fifteen degrees to the left. The seasoned group of pilots behind me adjusted to the shift and continued to fly in perfect formation without any radio signal or command. The major slammed his fists on top of the instrument panel. I flinched, but kept on flying. I had just committed a grievous act, disobeying orders in combat. Knowing I could be court-martialed because of my insubordination, I hoped that I could convince a military court that I did the right thing. I believed that I made the right decision. The intercom was silent the entire way home.

Not sure if this would be my last flight on *Miss Prudy*, I gave it everything I had. I greased the landing—it was one of my better ones—and taxied slowly and cautiously to the hardstand where our ground crew chief waited for us. He gave us a thumbs up, but I couldn't acknowledge him under the watchful eyes of the major. I cut the engines, shed my gear, and followed the major down the escape hatch where Colonel Creer was waiting for us. Creer walked toward us with a spring in his step, reached out and grabbed my right hand in a firm handshake, "Alling," he said, "another great job. Nice going!" Creer addressed both of us: "Come on guys, hop in the car. I want you to see the photos." Pointing to the back seat, "Alling, you ride in the back with me."

The major rode in the front with the driver, looking straight ahead. I never had a chance to make eye contact with my crew. I suppose they stood there in silence watching this turn of events. Nothing was ever mentioned of my insubordination. The major never flew with me again; in fact, we never crossed paths at the air base. I trust he understood that it was not my intention to challenge his authority, but to protect the men flying with me.

After the debriefing, I found Ray and Bill, "Thanks guys. You saved my ass." Later on, I met up with Jim Sain, another lead pilot. "Jim," I said, "I'll buy you a drink in Ipswich tonight if you are not flying tomorrow."

"You've got a deal," he replied.

On the way, we met up with Captain Daniels. With just two missions to go, Daniels was soon heading home. We asked him to join us, and that evening we reviewed my incident with the major.

"Did I do the right thing?" I asked my friends.

"Is there any doubt?" they answered as one.

The next morning, Bill showed up at the hut after breakfast with two-day passes for each of us. "Let's go to Stratford-on-Avon," he said. "I've always wanted to go to Shakespeare's home and I'm sure we can get tickets for a play."

We went to London first. After a late dinner, I went upstairs to read and Bill left for a short walk. When he returned, he had another one for me: "A beggar came up to me and asked for a thousand pounds. I told him it was a lot and he said, 'I'm putting all my begs in one asking'." The next day we boarded a train, getting off near the Shakespeare Memorial Theater. We purchased tickets for the evening performance of "Much Ado About Nothing" and found rooms at the William and Mary Hotel.

The next morning, Bill and I were having breakfast at the inn. The dining room was full, the mood somber, and the conversations in hushed tones. Two waitresses came over and offered their condolence. "We feel so sorry for you." Bill and I looked at each other, confused. "Your president died yesterday," they explained.

Franklin Delano Roosevelt died in Warm Springs, Georgia. It was a terrible misfortune that the president died before he had a chance to witness the end of hostilities and the final Allied victory. As we walked away from the dining room, an American dressed in army uniform approached us, "I saw you fellows in the dining room and have to say something to you. I'm here on Rest and Rehabilitation just back from the front, where I served as Forward Artillery Observer. If only you could see the smiles of the American troops as you soared overhead, all your efforts would be rewarded."

Mission of 19 April 194

Ref Base Wind 340 degrees; 35 knots
Ref Base Alt 20,000' Zero Hr 0800DB&T

* COMMUNICATIONS *

Wg Gnd Sta	Dusty Pink	A
Div Gnd Sta	Arrowswift	B
Div Collective	Highroad	B

Scouting Force:
Assy a/c	Kodak Control	B
Rte & Tgt Wx	Kodak Red	B
Base & Rte Wx	Drowsy D-Dog	B

Kodak Wx Code: I.P. – 10; Tgt – 11

Fiter-Bomber Communications:
Fiter Callsign	Balance 2-3	C
Bomber Callsing	Vinegrove 2-6	C
Fiter Gnd Sect	Colgate	C
Free Lance Fiters	Wabash 1, 2, 3	C
Div Authenticator	Theater	B
Div Recall Phrase	Madison Square Garden	B
Wg Recall Phrase	The Broadmoor Hotel	A
8AF Emerg Fixer(Cont)	Nuthouse	D
9AF Emerg Homer(Cont)	Vermont	D

* COLORS OF THE DAY *

TIME	FLARE	LETTER
0200-0800	YY	M – Mike
0800-1400	RRR	W – William
1400-2000	RR	H – How
2000-0200	RY	Y – Yoke

EMERGENCY AIRFIELDS:

B-53 (Merville) 5037-0239E, DOMESTIC D/N
  c/s DOMESTIC on darby command.
  Duncher: SUG on 1130 Kc.
Y-83 (Limburg) 5021-0804,

GEOGRAPHICAL REFERENCE POINTS & FITERS
B – Brunswick	Callsigns:
H – Wittenburg	
C – Berlin	BALANCE 2-3
R – Dresden	
T – Pilzen	VINEGROVE 2-6
E – Regensburg	
N – Leipzig	

WABASH ONE, TWO & THREE – Free lance
  Fiters giving area support.
Fiters giving support to this Gp have
  GREEN and YELLOW checkered noses.

PENETRATION – WITHDRAWAL CODE:
Plan 1 – Katie	Plan 4 – Helen
2 – Betty	5 – Flossie
3 – Dorothy	

Time on oxygen 2:30
Time over enemy territory 3:00
Time last T/O 0930 , intercept 7°E at
  6,000'

4th "A" Sq – LEAD (93 "B" Gp)

MAJ HERSH
ALLING – CAPT ZICK
231 H/H (9)

"D" BUCHANAN	FOX
183 B/K (15)	113 H/D
"C" PIERCE	RAYMOLD
929 B/Q (13)	840 B/E (16)
(*WILLIAMS	EDWARDS	(*GOLDING	(*TE...
953 B/D	950 B/L	331 B/Y	933
(17)	(17)	(17)	(1

Stations	0605	Taxi	0700
Alert	0610	Code	Texas
S/Engines	0645	Takeoff	0710
Code	Podunk	Assy Alt	6,000

34th "B" Sq – HIGH

HICKS – CAPT DANIELS
921 H/B (10)

"D" MARTIN, S	MARTIN, R
391 B/J (4)	237 H/I (10)
(* FERARD	COHEN
285 B/E (2)	280 B/M (3)
STENCH (* SCHROEDER	SCHWARTZ BEAUCHAMP
939 B/P 465 B/O	822 B/B(7) 325 B/B
(4) (3)	(* HAVSTER (6)
	367 B/L (6)

Stations	0605	Taxi	0600
Alert	0610	Code	Michigan
S/Engines	0635	Takeoff	0700
Code	Utopia	Assy Alt	6,500 ft

34th "C" Sq – LOW

HALL – CAPT BROWN
176 H/Q (6)

"B" ARAND	EVANS
271 L/O (18)	441 H/S (8)
BASS	
887 L/G (19)	
(*GRISHAM	DeLAIN
580 L/E (22)	257 L/T (19)
(* WORTH	
(Lflts) 243 L/I (19)	
FELDMAN	KRAMSCHUSTER
789 L/F (21)	864 L/B (18)
(*BAKER	
372 L/A (22)	

Stations	0605	Taxi	0710
Alert	0610	Code	California
S/Engines	0655	Takeoff	0720
Code	Fantasia	Assy Alt	5,500 ft

GROUND SPARES: G.I.'s:
PFF (1) 457 B/G (11)   332 L/Q (21)
  (2) 829 H/B (9)   410 B/H (17)
(*) – Camera a/c   334 H/D (1)
STAND BY CREWS: RAWSON (18) MASON (391)

S E C R E T

Secret flight plan for mission over Aussig, April 19, 1945.

His words were terrific to hear and a testimony to the Eighth Air Force.

Years later, I learned that when a German soldier heard a B-17 flying overhead, he ducked. It was different for American soldiers; the roar of the bombers was the "music of angels."[29]

April 19, 1945   With the Russians now fighting for Berlin, the American high command was concerned that the Nazis would try to regroup for a last stand in the mountainous south. We were ordered back to Czechoslovakia on another ten-hour roundtrip. This mission is embedded in Bill Wright's memory:

> At 4:50 A.M. the sergeant pushed open the door of our hut. "All right men, out of the sack! Hit the bricks!" My feet hit the cold floor. We already knew we were going to be "up" that day. Being up was a dangerous and exhausting job, but somebody had to do it, and we were good at it. But why did we close down the Officer's Club last night? The last thing I remember was the club officer turning the owl on the mantle, and then I knew it was time to leave.
>
> I'm getting tired of this, getting up while it is still black dark, cold and damp while most sane people are still curled up in the sack. We all know the Krauts are on their last legs and that the war will end before long. Will this be our last mission? Where will we be going today, and will we return? All of us? What a terrible waste it will be if we don't make it back after all we've been through.
>
> The briefing room was quiet as Colonel Creer greeted us, and introduced us to a captain who proceeded to tell us about the day's mission.
>
> "Gentlemen, your mission today is to a place you've probably never heard of—Aussig, Czechoslovakia. It's located about twenty miles from the German border and thirty miles due north of Prague. Our target is a large, active marshalling yard built in two sections connected by a railroad bridge. This facility is vital to Germany—it's being used to funnel supplies south to the German armies desperately trying to hold a front

against the Russians. Now the Russians are coming from the east and the Allies will push toward Berlin from the west. It is a perfect, well-identified target that should not present bombardiers with a problem. There is the possibility of some fighters near the target, but no flak whatsoever. Our bombing altitude will be fifteen thousand feet. Each plane will be carrying six 1,000-pound general purpose bombs. Estimated flying time is ten hours and thirty minutes. This will be one of the longest missions of the war."

"Captain Alling," he continued. (Now I had to listen intently; I flew with Captain Alling.) "Your crew will be flying group lead today. Colonel Hershenow will fly with you as command pilot. And Captain Alling, he needs to meet with you right now for a special briefing."

Chuck left for another briefing room and our instructions continued. "Navigators will meet with Captain Metz and bombardiers will meet with Captain Crook for further briefing. God speed and good luck, men!"

The final bombing mission of the Miss Prudy *crew was clearly remembered by its bombardier Bill Wright.* (USAAF)

We had flown with Colonel Hershenow before. I knew he was a fine pilot and to his credit he had flown many combat missions. We gathered our gear and thermal suits and headed to the jeep assigned to deliver us to *Miss Prudy*. Not a word was spoken on our ride to the hardstand; there was only enough time for last thoughts and prayers.

Miss Prudy was waiting for us. The ground crew took meticulous care of her and she was ready to fly. They greeted us with a warm smile and a hint of anxiety they were trying to restrain. Now they will have to wait patiently for our return, sweating it out until we make it back in one piece.

I climbed on board and checked the bombsight, making sure it had been installed properly, and checked to see if the on/off switch in the gyro (the stabilizer in the base of the bombsight) was working. I set all the data I received at the briefing along with information I obtained from the charts and tables provided. I checked the ground temperature, barometric pressure, estimated temperature and pressure at bombing altitude, along with the wind speed and the directions for the target area. I checked my thermal suit connections, mike hookup, oxygen mask, and temporary oxygen supply bottle.

A fuel truck pulled up alongside *Miss Prudy* to top-off her tanks, giving us every gallon she could hold—and then some. You never knew what was in store in each flight. This may be a long mission, and we may need every drop of fuel we've got, making little room for error.

I prayed that the bomb group got off to a good start. We'd had enough anxious takeoffs and long tedious hours of assembly time with hundreds of planes flying in the clouds, their contrails gradually covering the sky like a giant curtain.

I imagined what this bomb run would be like. Soon I would be crouching over the bombsight in painful anticipation of what lay ahead. The outside thermometer would read minus fifty degrees Centigrade, and it would be so cold inside that if my thermal suit malfunctioned, I would freeze to death. With growing tension, I waited for Ray's command, "Seven minutes to I.P. and five more to target."

For me, that meant twelve minutes of hell. And finally,

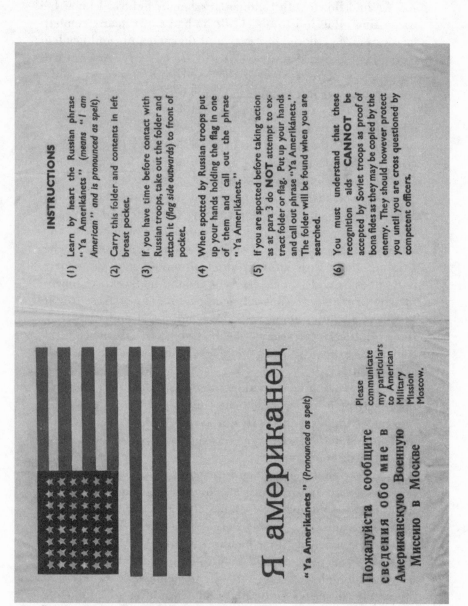

INSTRUCTIONS

(1) Learn by heart the Russian phrase "Ya Amerikánets" (means "I am American" and is pronounced as spelt).

(2) Carry this folder and contents in left breast pocket.

(3) If you have time before contact with Russian troops, take out the folder and attach it (flag side outwards) to front of pocket.

(4) When spotted by Russian troops put up your hands holding the flag in one of them and call out the phrase "Ya Amerikánets."

(5) If you are spotted before taking action as at para 3 do NOT attempt to extract folder or flag. Put up your hands and call out phrase "Ya Amerikánets." The folder will be found when you are searched.

(6) You must understand that these recognition aids CANNOT be accepted by Soviet troops as proof of bona fides as they may be copied by the enemy. They should however protect you until you are cross questioned by competent officers.

Я американец

"Ya Amerikánets" (Pronounced as spelt)

Пожалуйста сообщите сведения обо мне в Американскую Военную Миссию в Москве

Please communicate my particulars to American Military Mission Moscow.

Leaflet given to members of all the bomber crews that flew to Czechoslovakia near the Russian lines, April 19, 1945. (USAAF)

"Bombs away!" That's what we came for, after all. But it still would not be over. We would make a turn to the right from the target to lead the pack home.

Sometimes the trip home was the worst part. Our planes were torn apart by enemy fire, smoking, burning, engines out, props feathered, some heading down to the ground, completely out of control, some lagging behind, no longer able to keep up with the formation, and knowing they're sitting ducks for the 109s flying overhead. Sometimes we saw chutes, but most of the time there were none. But we had a great pilot to lead this crew of young men who were living on the edge, scared to death. We were doing our best, our very best.

I had been in deep thought, almost a trance. Now, it was time to leave, and we were off. The flight was smooth as we flew to our first rendezvous point in the assembly procedure. We were leading the 34th Bomb Group. I would not want to have been Ray. He had the responsibility of guiding the 34th through an ever growing sea of contrails from hundreds of bombers jockeying for position in the bomber stream; but Ray had a genius for leading us from radio buncher to buncher on course and on time. An error of a few hundred feet or a few seconds in time could have been disastrous.

We continued to climb in an ever-tightening formation at the constant rate of three hundred feet per minute. We reached eight thousand feet at our ECO (English coast out) marker and we headed out on a course that took us safely to the target more than four hours away. Ray's course took us a few miles south of the target. Then only one turn lead us directly to the I.P.

So far, the mission had been easy. The sky was clear, and we encountered very little flak. I could see miles and miles of peaceful countryside below, and small towns, the names of which we will never know. The city of Dresden loomed in the distance to the north. Along our route, we were on radio silence, and all was quiet except for the hum of our engines.

"Seven minutes to I.P.," said Ray. I was almost startled to hear his voice. I acknowledged him. Silence again.

"Approaching I.P.," Ray directed us. I had a perfect picture of the target thirty miles straight ahead of us. With a favorable wind behind us, our ground speed was 215 knots. It was time to line up the target.

"Bomb bay doors are open," I called out.

"You've got it. It's all yours," said Chuck. "Good luck, guy!"

The lateral control of the plane was now mine. We were twenty miles from the target. I lined the vertical hair with the target, and I held it there by slightly maneuvering the plane to the left or right as needed. Then I picked up the target in the crosshair and adjusted the sight to hold it there. I knew I would be making constant, minor adjustments, holding the vertical and crosshairs on the target perfectly still. I started to feel confident and believed we would have a good run.

The Norden bombsight was now in control, making line-of-sight calculations, the indices slowly coming together, and it was out of my hands, too late for any more adjustments. Ten seconds until bomb drop—nine, eight, seven, six . . . the

Aerial photo of bombs from author's unit hitting the railroad marshalling yards in Aussig, Czechoslovakia, April 19, 1945. (USAAF)

indices came together at the count of one. The bombs dropped in salvo and exploded directly on the target.

Chuck was now back in control of the plane and made a turn to the right to head back to Mendlesham. As we banked slowly and cautiously, I could not help but think of innocent civilians. We had hit the target beautifully, but how many people—men, women and children, most of them uninvolved in this terrible matter, had just been killed or maimed? Just then—that moment—how many were dying?

Again, all was quiet except for the roar of hundreds of engines in the squadron until I heard Glen: "Chuck, I can see fighter planes on the field below. The planes were being towed by horses to the runway."

I knew it wouldn't be long before we would see them in the sky above and beyond us. "Keep an eye on them," I replied.

A minute later, Glen returned to the intercom. "Twelve fighter planes have just taken off."

"OK guys, let's get ready. Bandits on the way," I called into the intercom, hoping to exude confidence.

Seconds later, I heard Jack Brame's rattled voice, "Twelve jets at 3 o'clock high! Look out! Bandits at 3 o'clock high!"

I saw the Luftwaffe fighters banking left so as to approach us dead on. I turned into their turn, forcing them into a tighter bank, thereby reducing the actual time they had to shoot tracers at us. It was a deadly synchronization, cutting their time to fire while our group's gunners opened up. Guns blazed and the sky seemed to shudder with the horrifying and deafening sounds of hundreds of machine guns firing from all directions. The dozen Me 262's bore into us at over 500 mph, their cannon blinking. Colonel Hershenow instinctively ducked his head below the window. My crew gave it their all and fired rapidly into the approaching formation. Their first element of four flew at and over us, and then there was a two second break before the second and then the third elements passed underneath.

"My God!" said Colonel Hershenow as he peeked over the panel. "Nice maneuver, Alling!"

"It's okay now. I don't think they'll be back," I said.

A minute later, Glen, in his observer's position in the rear, came on the intercom, "Germans just blew up four B-17s in the 470th bomb group behind us, and further back, there are several explosions. I can't tell if it's us or them."

"Any chutes?" I asked, wondering if any of us knew the crew on board those four B-17s.

"No chutes," Glen replied. I knew he hated to be the one to report the loss of four B-17s as another forty young men had just died. No one wants to see a plane go down; a part of us goes down with them.

Bill described the ride home from there:

> The trip home seemed as peaceful as our trip to the target. The sky above was filled with our Little Friends. Our visibility was clear and we could see some of the targets we bombed in the weeks past. We flew directly over Hof where our bombs had fallen short, the Ruhr valley, and the industrial cities of Dusseldorf, Bonn and Koblenz, their factories now silenced. As we passed over Belgium, we were careful not to fly over small pockets of fanatical resistance along the coast.

This was Colonel Hershenow's thirtieth and final mission. If we were to get back safely, he would be heading home to a new command, probably in the States. He reached over and tapped me on the shoulder, "Captain Alling, this is my last mission. Would you mind if I buzz the tower and make the landing?"

I smiled and took my hands off the wheel. "All yours, Colonel!"

He broke into a broad smile, "Do you think when we fly over the airfield that we can shoot off some flares, too?" he said.

"Colonel," I replied, "we'll shoot every flare we can find!" It was customary for crews that had finished their tour to fire up flares as they buzzed the field. This was the colonel's moment in the limelight and he deserved every bit of it. Hershenow swooped down the runway with Willie Green shooting every flare he could get his hands on. I knew the ground crew and the support teams at the base loved this. The officers in the control tower loved it, too, for they knew that one more man or one more crew had just completed their tour of duty.

Hershenow circled the field, making a wide turn until he was lined up with the landing approach. As he started down, I called off the airspeed, "140, 135, 130." I knew that he should be touching down at this moment, but he was flying too high and too fast. Hershenow was going to overshoot the runway and he knew it. He yanked the throttles as far back as he could and the plane dropped. I thought we were going to blow the tires. Fortunately, we did not. *Miss Prudy* kept rolling forward, with full flaps down, right off the end of the runway and settled into the mud. Hershenow's face, once bright with joy, was stunned and distracted. I smiled to reassure him and shook his hand. "Colonel Hershenow, any landing you can walk away from is a good landing."

We eased our way down the escape hatch into the mud. Colonel Creer was standing at the edge of the runway waiting for us. We

Crew of Miss Prudy following their last bombing mission over Aussig, Czechoslovakia, April 19, 1945. Left to right, standing: 1st Lieutenant Bill Wright, 1st Lieutenant Ray Baskin, Captain Chuck Alling, 1st Lieutenant Glen Banks. Left to right, kneeling: T/Sgt. Jack Brame, T/Sgt. Eddie Edwards, T/Sgt. Willie Green, T/Sgt. Chuck Williams. (USAAF)

stepped gingerly, sinking into the mud on our way to greet him. Creer could not refrain himself from laughing, "Alling, when are you going to learn how to fly a plane?"

He turned and shook hands with Colonel Hershenow, put his hand on his shoulder and said, "Congratulations, Bill, but tell me, who really made that landing?" Hershenow started to explain but Creer interrupted, "Never mind, I figured as much. We have reports in from the other groups that twelve Messerschmitts hit our group and missed. You did a fine job in the 34th—all your planes survived. Unfortunately, the Germans got six B-17s in groups behind you. We shot down seven of theirs—hardly a fair exchange."

Bill described how he concluded that day:

> By the time we got to the debriefing, Intelligence officers had photos of our target on the screen. Everyone in the room was smiling. "A great job! Great job!" the officers assured us.
>
> General Gerhard, our wing commander, added, "Your rating for this mission is very good! Congratulations men!"
>
> Colonel Creer stepped forward, "Captain Alling, I am recommending you and your crew for the Distinguished Flying Cross."
>
> Later, I walked slowly into our Nissen hut, tired and cold—always cold. Putting a few pieces of coal on the fire, I pulled off my shoes and jacket and walked over to my bunk in the corner. I sat there thinking about the day and wondering what tomorrow would bring.
>
> Every man needs his space and this corner was mine. On a makeshift table beside the bunk, there was an old cigar box where I kept all my treasures: an old pipe with a half full can of Prince Albert; an extra pair of dog tags; a small coin which a little girl in Gymmeppe, Belgium, gave me several months ago when her family befriended me after my first B-17 bomber had been shot down; and, a piece of flak that I had found on Ray's desk after a mission to Merseburg when *Miss Prudy* was sprayed with bullets. And there were reminders from home: a note about my twin brother who was honored with two Purple Hearts in Italy; a picture of my mother, who was always my best friend; a St. Christopher's medal my mother had given me; and perhaps the most precious of all, a photograph of my

beautiful wife, Nell. We had been married in the post chapel at Ellington Field just eight months before.

I took the photograph of Nell in my hand, and a thousand thoughts rushed through my head. Will I ever see her again? What will happen to her if I don't make it back? What about all our plans and dreams? I gently lifted the photograph of the person I loved deeply, more than life, and held it gently just as if I were holding her. Then I placed the photograph carefully back in the box, closing it tightly to protect everything inside. For now, we were together. For now, we were both safe.

JOY AND SORROW

Sullen skies today,
Sunny skies tomorrow;
November steals from May,
And May from her doth borrow;
Griefs – Joys – in Time's strange dance
Interchangeably advance;
The sweetest joys that come to us
Come sweeter for past sorrow.

—Aubrey De Vere[30]

11

Many Thanks, Yanks

⬩⬩⬩

The air strike over Aussig, Czechoslovakia, was our twenty-seventh mission, and it was also the last aerial engagement in World War II between the Eighth Air Force and the Luftwaffe. On April 29, 1945, the fascist dictator Mussolini was captured and killed by partisans near Lake Como, a picture-perfect little town in northern Italy. To the south, sloping hills descend gracefully to the lake's edge with cone-shaped cypress trees trailing the landscape. To the north, peaks rise from the water, and fishing villages and harbors are nestled into the hills. To the east, the Swiss Alps rise above the lake with snow-covered crests. Mussolini and his mistress were hanged from their heels at a filling station.

The next day, April 30, Adolf Hitler gave his new wife and long-time mistress, Eva Braun, a poison pill and then he shot himself. Russian troops were by then closing in on his bunker in a Berlin that had been blasted beyond recognition by Allied bombers. Hitler had ordered his body to be burned and buried so that it would not become a Russian trophy.

⬩⬩⬩

At the time, word was coming by underground wireless from Holland that Dutch civilians were starving to death at the rate of a thousand a day in the German-occupied areas. Germany had held the major cities and had confiscated the food. The Dutch had to resort to eating their cats and dogs. They begged the Germans for grain to no avail and resorted to eating tulip bulbs for nourishment. The winter had been terribly cold, and without blankets and coal they had wrapped themselves in rugs at night to keep warm. Help was desperately needed and the Dutch could not possibly wait for hostilities to end. Until now, the Allies had avoided civilian areas occupied by German troops, because of the intense concentration of artillery and antiaircraft guns. By the end of April, however, the Allies and Germans had entered into negotiations to set up food drops for the Dutch. These negotiations were documented by Dutch historian Walter Maass and they progressed as follows:

> For several weeks, the International Red Cross had worked to broker a deal with the Germans, British and Americans. The relief negotiations were held at a school at Achterveld [a village just within the Allied front line near Amersfoort]. General Eisenhower was represented by General Bedell-Smith, Montgomery by General De Guingaud. Also present were Prince Bernhard and a Russian officer. The German negotiators arrived by car, were stopped at some distance from the meeting place, and proceeded on foot under a white flag. Both parties had brought their experts for organizing the relief work. [Nazi commissioner for the Netherlands] Seyss-Inquart was accompanied by the Dutch Food Commissioner, Louwes . . .
>
> Discussions started, with the participants facing each other at a large table. Again, Seyss-Inquart rejected unconditional surrender, because such a step would hurt him in the final judgement of history. An argument began between him and Bedell-Smith and the latter impatiently exclaimed: "Come on, speak up! You know you'll be shot anyway!"
>
> Seyss-Inquart replied, "That leaves me cold."
>
> Whereupon the American scoffed, "It certainly will!"[31]

At the close of the negotiations, six food drops were scheduled to take place in early May. The parties agreed to a five-hour truce during which the Eighth Air Force was allowed to fly over Holland without being shot at by the Germans. The American planes would carry a full crew, without ammunition, fly on a predetermined route, and drop cartons of food at designated drop zones. It was agreed that if a bomber strayed out of the safe corridor, the Germans would shoot blanks as a warning.

May 1, 1945 We were briefed for the first mercy mission, known by some as a "chow haul," to Rotterdam, Holland. We were told the Dutch were starving to death; every dog, cat, and vermin had been eaten. The Dutch had even stripped and burned the wood inside their homes to stay warm. The underground radio reported that relief planes would be coming but the message was met with doubt. Who had ever heard of planes dropping food parcels in a territory occupied by the enemy? No one imagined the Germans would permit it.

John K. Gerhart, commanding general of the 93rd Bomb Wing (which included four bomb groups), was to fly with Captain Delmar Dunham. Dunham led four hundred planes of the Eighth Air Force. We were assigned to fly deputy lead, with Colonel Creer as our command pilot.

We were to fly into Rotterdam at three to four hundred feet and drop "ten-in-one" rations of canned meat, butter, bread, jam, and sacks of flour wrapped in heavy burlap secured by thin steel straps. The drop zones were marked by large red crosses in open fields, parks, race tracks, and an airfield.[32]

The Supreme Headquarters Allied Expeditionary Forces (SHAEF) had given the go-ahead to begin the food drops, and we did not know that the final agreement for the delivery of food was not signed until May 2. That meant the first mercy mission began a day before the agreement was official. If we had known, we would have been far more concerned flying into Rotterdam without ammunition, even though we understood the Germans were not to fire at us.

We assembled at one thousand feet and left England, passing over Felixstowe on the way, and a hundred miles from the coast of Britain we reached Holland. We descended to four hundred feet as we approached Rotterdam. As we flew over the city, I looked down for only a few seconds. We were in tight formation off the general's right wing, and there were hundreds of planes behind us. In those moments, I captured a glimpse of the unfolding drama that will rest in my mind forever.

As we approached the drop zone, I realized there were thousands of people lining the streets, leaning out of their windows, and watching from the roof tops. I saw a sea of white; everything was white except for an occasional splash of color. The Dutch were waving anything white they could get their hands on—sheets, handkerchiefs, scarves, towels, and some waved the American flag. Men, women,

Mercy Mission Chow Haul & retrieving prisoners

SECRET   Mission of 1st May, 1945.

34A CLAMBAKE SUGAR LEADER (RR)

Had time with Germans till 11:00
Led wing (our group) 400 ships

DUNHAM-GEN. GERHART
556 H/F (11)MAJ PRATT
ALLING-COL CREER *500 tons of 10 in 1*
829 H/B(9)CAPT ROGERS *rations*

"B" THOMANDER
280 E/M (3)

FERARD
416 B/C (2)

COUSE
179 B/A (7)

STEMEN "C₈"
939 E/P (3)

MUELLER
334 E/D (1)

Stations	0640
Alert	0645
St. Engs.	0710
Code	CHICAGO
Taxi	0725
Code	ILLINOIS
T.O.	0730
Assy Alt.	1,500

34B Clambake Sugar Baker (YY)

Alt 400-900 feet

HANCHAR-CAPT STEWART
921 H/R (10) LT ANTHONY

"B" HAVENER
367 E/L (6)

MARTIN, S.
325 E/B (5)

MC CUTCHAN
286 E/T (2)

SCHROEDER
320 E/G (1)

SCHWARTZ
309 E/H (6)

BALZER
253 E/N (4)

Stations	0640
Alert	0645
St. Engs.	0715
Code	DAYTON
Taxi	0730
Code	OHIO
T.O.	0735
Assy Alt.	1,000

logged 4:20
Enemy terr.
1:30
Saw people
waving arms!

34C CLAMBAKE SUGAR CHARLIE (RG)

Dutch surrender flags.

CARMAN-CAPT ZICK
670 H/K (8)

"B" HACK
326 B/U (15)

FOX
183 B/K (15)

NOVICKI
933 B/C (14)

GOLDING
331 B/Y (17)

BUCHANAN
216 B/O (13)

FIEDLER
321 B/F (13)

Stations	0640
Alert	0645
St. Engs.	0720
Code	ALBANY
Taxi	0735
Code	NEW YORK
T.O.	0740
Assy Alt.	1,500

800 foot ceiling all day.

Rotterdam

34D CLAMBAKE SUGAR DOG (RY)

took tree returned by Jerries.

MOORE-CAPT DANIELS
210 B/H (17) Lt. Gulli

GULMETTI
960 B/L (17)

PIERRE
327 L/R (20)

WILLIAMS
953 B/D (17)

AGEGIAN
282 B/V (13)

BUCKHOLZ
409 B/B (15)

RAWSON
373 B/J (14)

Stations	0640
Alert	0645
St. Engs.	0725
Code	MIAMI
Taxi	0740
Code	FLORIDA
T.O.	0745
Assy Alt.	1,000

Red + ships in harbor

34E CLAMBAKE SUGAR EASY (GG)

HALL - CAPT VIAR
959 L/H (22) LT VAN LIERE

GAST
138 L/J (18)

TYSON
789 L/F (21)

SYKES
378 L/K (20)

HINKLE
864 L/E (21)

DWYER
343 L/I (19)

Stations	0640
Alert	0645
St. Engs.	0730
Code	DALLAS
Taxi	0745
Code	TEXAS
T.O.	0750
Assy Alt.	1,500

34F CLAMBAKE SUGAR FOX (QY)

HICKS-CAPT SIMONS
822 E/E (7) LT BRYANT

RIDER
299 L/U (19)

CONRAD
271 L/O (18)

EVANS
372 L/A (22)

MASON
380 L/B (22)

GREGORY
382 L/Q (21)

Stations	0640
Alert	0645
St. Engs.	0735
Code	BOSTON
Taxi	0750
Code	MASSACHUSETTS
T.O.	0755
Assy Alt.	1,000

GROUND SPARES: Feldman (391st); Hunt(18th); Beauchamp (7th) Over base or "FELIX-
PERTINENT POOP: ZERO HOUR 0745   LAST TIME OF T/O 0800 R/V AT STOWE
REF. BASE ALT. 1,000
REF. BASE WIND 340° - 20k   TIME OVER ENEMY TERR. 50 Min

SECRET

Flight plan for food drop over Holland, May 1, 1945.

and children were full of excitement and joy, cheering, clapping, and dancing while German gunners leaned against the barrels of their 88mm cannons. If a German had dared to shoot, I believe he would have been trampled to death by the Dutch.

Up ahead I could see the drop zone in a field, and as we approached there was a surging mass of people. We had to drop our food quickly and expeditiously to avoid any accidental casualties. There were brave, elderly citizens trying to hold back an exultant crowd.

"Bombs away!" called Bill, and *Miss Prudy* bounced up as cartons of food were released.

We gradually gained altitude and slowly banked to the left, heading toward the English Channel as I flew off Dunham's right wing in close formation. As we left Rotterdam, other groups in the fleet of B-17s were still making their way in, each one a part of this mercy mission.

Not far from the coast of England, I was conscious that I was tiring. My left wrist was numb—I had been flying in tight formation for hours without relief. Suddenly, Dunham's plane swerved to the right unexpectedly. Colonel Creer, alert and nimble, grabbed the wheel, turning away just in time to avoid a mid-air collision. Dunham straightened out and we quickly returned to our formation. "Thank you, Colonel Creer, my hands are numb. I can't feel the steering wheel—I can't grip it anymore."

"Alling, why don't you let me fly the plane to the base? I'm sorry I didn't spell you sooner. I got so carried away with the sight below us that I forgot to share the load with you."

May 3, 1945 We were briefed for our second mercy mission, the third launched by the Eighth Air Force in that first week of May. This flight would take us over Amsterdam. We were the lead plane of the Eighth Air Force with Lieutenant Colonel Ed Freeman, 18th Squadron commander, as our command pilot. We received instructions to fly single file over the city to ensure the accuracy of the food drop on the designated red cross zones.

As we approached the continent, the weather turned sour and it began to rain. I knew the poor visibility would make the accuracy of this drop challenging. As we were the first to approach Amsterdam, I flew in at three hundred feet off the ground with the 34th Bomb

Above: *A low-flying B-17 releases its cargo over Holland for the relief of the starving country. Eight hundred tons of food was dropped during the first three days of May 1945.*
(The New York Times)

Inset: *Food dropping from plane over Holland.* (USAAF)

Group behind me. Over the city I dipped my wings to alert the Germans not to shoot. I wondered if every German soldier would heed this armistice; if one fired, we would be the first to go. For a few moments it was tense, but once I believed the Germans would keep their commitment, we searched for the drop zone. Without a break in the clouds and continued poor visibility, we had to circle the city and make another pass. As we approached, Bill called in, "Chuck, I can't see the target!"

"Okay, we're going to do a 360," I replied.

As Colonel Freeman informed the rest of the command pilots, I knew he was becoming anxious. This assignment was turning out to be more difficult than expected with poor visibility, limited time, limited gas supply, and hundreds more planes of the Eighth Air Force coming up behind us. With each and every minute that we were unable to drop the food, this mission became increasingly complex.

Eight minutes later, we approached the city for another pass. Bill called, "Bomb bay doors open! Flaps down!" I felt a sense of relief knowing the food drop would take place any moment. With the flaps down, it gave *Miss Prudy* the lift she needed as our true ground speed was 140 miles per hour, and we couldn't go any slower or we'd stall out. We were now three hundred feet off the ground. Just moments before the drop, Bill called on the intercom, "Chuck, I still can't see anything!"

Now we were in real trouble. "All right," I said, "Let's circle and we'll try again." I gave Freeman the signal. Thirty-eight planes followed us around the city once more. I took a deep breath.

As we circled Amsterdam, Bill said, "Chuck, we've got to try this one more time, and this time we have to fly as low as we possibly can without stalling out!" Bill was agitated.

"How much lower do you think we can go?" I asked, wondering if this food drop was possible.

"Drop to two hundred feet," Bill called, "But for God's sake don't go any lower!"

This would have to be our final attempt, and I certainly could not fly any lower unless we wanted to wrap ourselves around a tree or a windmill. I was exasperated and worried. As we flew back over Amsterdam, I thought of all the Dutch who were starving and desperate for relief. If we could not find the drop zone, there would be chaos in the streets.

"There it is!" Bill yelled, unleashing all his pent-up tension. "I can see the cross! Bombs away!" Bill pulled the switch and cartons of food fell to the earth.

For those watching from below, I can only imagine the sight of hundreds of B-17s flying into the city at a dangerously low level. The noise of the engines must have been deafening as five hundred bombers flew over Amsterdam, one after the next, every thirty seconds, for three and a half hours, dropping thousands of cartons of food.

I looked down for a few seconds. There were thousands of people running in the streets with their white handkerchiefs, white cloth, white flags, anything white. And then I focused on something I will never forget. There was a gray-haired gentleman with a wooden peg-leg, swinging a cane, and hobbling in the direction of the food. A little girl with long blonde hair, who must have been his granddaughter, was restraining him with all her might. She leaned back, her heels dug into the soil, pulling on his coattails to keep him from moving forward into the falling cartons of food.

Ray saw people standing behind glass doors waving, a cow tumble and fall as it was hit by a carton of food, and a funeral cortege of horses that pulled a caisson with the casket on it, the mourners walking behind clutching flowers. Sometimes it's the odd things that remain fixed in our memory.

During the first three days in May alone, eight hundred tons of food were dropped over Holland, enough to provide 1,080,000 meals. The mercy missions were a massive undertaking and unprecedented in wartime history.

<hr />

Seven years later, I was invited to join a group of marketing executives on a European trip organized by the Departments of State and Commerce and the U.S. Sales Executive Association. I was one of eight executives traveling to ten European countries. We flew to Scandinavia, Holland, France, England, Scotland, and Ireland.

When we arrived in Amsterdam, I went for a walk with my wife, Gail. I was delighted to see so many Dutch living life to its fullest. During our first night in Amsterdam, the American businessmen and their spouses were guests at a black-tie dinner for fifty at the Grand

Amstel Hotel. We were all seated at one large elliptical table, and the American ambassador sat next to us.

In Holland, it is the custom that toasts follow dinner. The burgomaster of Amsterdam was the first to rise to his feet. A stout man with white hair and a ruddy complexion, he began the first toast of the evening. "This is a night in my life I will cherish." He enjoyed holding the floor and continued, "By the spring of 1945, our cities were occupied by the Germans. My fellow citizens were faced with another foe—starvation. We had no food. German soldiers had confiscated our dairy and vegetable products. There was hardly a cow, horse, goat or chicken within hundreds of miles."

I quickly realized that someone in our group had leaked the story of our food drop. The burgomaster continued. "On May 3, 1945, I remember this day so well," and he paused with a deep breath. "My sister wrote to me, 'Unless a gift comes from Heaven, we will soon die. All we can do is hope and pray.' And then, as if to answer her prayers, I heard a noise outside that sounded like thunder. Looking out the window I could see, off in the distance, a line of bombers approaching Amsterdam. I saw the first plane flying in just above the treetops with a fleet of ships behind. She dipped her wings in her approach. I knew the significance of that friendly gesture. The Germans didn't shoot. They leaned on their cannons and watched.

"A number of B-17s circled the city a few times in a broad sweep, searching for the drop zone. The roar of the engines was thunderous, almost deafening, as the stream of bombers approached the city. Everyone ran outside to see. Then my wife and I, and many others, watched in total amazement, almost disbelief, as an armada of ships—these 'angels of mercy'—came across the horizon and flew into Amsterdam.[33] The ground seemed to shake as they flew over us. We waived to the American pilots and their crews. And then I couldn't believe what I saw. Each plane dropped cartons of food onto a field just up the road. We were crying with joy. I put both arms around my wife and I hugged and kissed her. We hugged and squeezed our neighbors. We, and thousands of others, were dancing in the streets. Everyone was delirious with joy! We were euphoric! We were, and are, forever grateful!"

I looked around the table nervously. Once again, I saw white—white handkerchiefs, white linen napkins—all reminders of that memorable sight, seven years earlier, as we flew over Amsterdam. The dinner guests were listening intently, their eyes filled with tears. Even my American colleagues wiped their eyes with their white linen napkins. And then with all the emotion he could muster, the burgomaster continued, "And, my friends, Charles Alling, the young American who led the mighty armada, is with us tonight!"

As if by command, the dinner guests rose to their feet in applause. It was time for me to speak. I rose to my feet slowly, frantically thinking about what I would say. Clearing my throat, I took a very deep breath. "Thank you Mr. Burgomaster. I'm so glad to see you're eating better today." Everyone laughed, which helped. I paused, and this time took a more relaxed breath. "Now, I have a story to tell you." Again I paused, and read the anticipation in their faces, noticing the chefs with their tall, white hats, the waiters, waitresses and the entire kitchen staff had entered the room to listen. "After the food drop, we flew over your beautiful country toward the sea. As we passed over fields of beautiful, yellow tulips, we saw the most extraordinary sight. You wonderful people had clipped the heads of the tulips to spell, 'MANY THANKS, YANKS'."

I sat down to a hush as if all the oxygen had evaporated from the room. Stunned by the warm silence, I picked my white napkin off the table and placed it carefully on my lap. No one moved. I looked around and felt as though embraced by the emotion on all their faces and their expressions of sincere gratitude for what the Americans had done for their country.

Sensing the need for another kind of relief, the burgomaster rose to his feet just in time. "Thank you, Captain Alling! Thank you!" he said joyfully. "And now we have a token of our appreciation for you!" And with that, a waiter handed a large box to the burgomaster, who walked around the table and presented it to me. I carefully untied the red, white, and blue striped ribbon. The white tissue crumbled and fell to the table, revealing a suspended parachute on top of the largest bottle I had ever seen. It had six compartments, each with a different liqueur. I shook hands with the burgomaster and those around me, and asked one of the taller waiters if he would serve each guest with the liqueur of their choice.

When I think of the Dutch and what they endured during the war, I feel nothing but respect. They are a people with great spirit.

They are survivors. They love life, and even when their families lay starving and dying, their spirit remained intact. The Germans could not tear apart the soul of this ravished country.

I still marvel at their task of clipping hundreds of tulips to create a message clearly visible to our planes hundreds of feet above the ground. This was not a small task for a nation of starving people, and it was a brave one for people fearing possible retribution. When I think about the mission over Amsterdam, I have a single, dramatic image in my mind of fields of yellow tulips, blossoming on the edge of devastation and war.

WE BREAK NEW SEAS TODAY

Each man is Captain of his Soul,
And each man his own Crew,
But the Pilot knows the Unknown Seas,
And he will bring us through.

We break new seas today –
Our eager keels quest unaccustomed waters,
And, from the vast uncharted waste in front,
The mystic circles leap
To greet our prows with mightiest possibilities,
Bringing us – What?

Dread shouls and shifting banks?
And calms and storms?
And clouds and biting gales?
And wreck and loss?
And valiant fighting times?
And, maybe, death! – and so, the Larger Life!

For, should the Pilot deem it best
To cut the voyage short,
He sees beyond the sky-line, and
He'll bring us to Port!

—John Oxenham[34]

12

Victory in Europe

————— ❖◆❖ —————

*M*ay 6, 1945   Grand Admiral Karl Doenitz, who had become head of the Third Reich after Hitler's death, authorized an official surrender to the Allies. The text of this order read "I authorize Colonel General Jodl, Chief of the Operations' Staff in the High Command of the Armed Forces, to conclude an armistice agreement with the headquarters of General Eisenhower."

The new German approach met the demands of the Allies for a total, unconditional surrender of all German forces on both the Western and Eastern fronts. Doenitz and other German leaders had hoped until the last minute to make a separate peace with the British and American armies while continuing to resist the Soviet advance in the East or at least making some arrangement whereby German troops could avoid surrendering to Soviet armies. These alternatives, clearly contrary to the spirit and letter of accords reached at summit conferences between the Big Three heads of government, were rejected out of hand by General Eisenhower, at whose insistence the first instruments of unconditional surrender were signed the following morning in Reims.[35]

The unconditional surrender of the German Third Reich was signed in the early morning hours of Monday, May 7, 1945; the time on the documents was noted as 2:41 A.M. The scene was the war room at SHAEF, located in the Professional and Technical School at Reims, a historic city in northeastern France that had been almost completely leveled by the Germans during the war.

Across the conference table, representatives of the four Allied powers—France, Great Britain, the Soviet Union, and the United States—faced the three German officers delegated by Doenitz: Colonel General Alfred Jodl, the head of Germany's Oberkommando der Wehrmacht (OKW), who alone had been authorized to sign the surrender document; General Admiral Hans Georg von Friedeburg, a chief negotiator, and Major Friedrich Wilhelm Oxenius, an aide to Jodl.

Lieutenant General Walter Bedell-Smith, SHAEF chief of staff, led the Allied delegation as the representative of General Eisenhower, who had refused to meet with the Germans until the surrender had been accomplished. Other American officers present were Major General Harold R. Bull and the head of the American strategic air forces in Europe, General Carl Spaatz.

British observers were Admiral Sir Harold Burrough, Lieutenant General Sir Fred Morgan (SHAEF deputy chief of staff), and Air Marshal J. M. Robb. Major General Ivan Sousloparov, head of the Soviet mission to France, represented the Soviet High Command; he was accompanied by Lieutenant Ivan Chermiaev and Senior Lieutenant Colonel Ivan Zenkovitch as interpreters. Representing the French chief of staff (General Alphonse Pierre Juin) was Major General Francois Sevez.

The surrender document was signed by Jodl, on behalf of the German High Command, and Bedell-Smith, representing Eisenhower as supreme commander of the Anglo-American forces. The Russian, Sousloparov, signed as a witness, fulfilling the Big Three agreement that Soviet representatives would take part in any ceremony of total surrender, and Sevez signed as a witness for France.[36] One of Eisenhower's stipulations, which the Germans had resisted to the last, was that a separate ceremony would take place on the Eastern front with the Germans formally surrendering to the Soviet Union.

Much has been written about Allied air power in World War II. In hindsight, the aerial war may have taken a different course if the Germans had mass produced the Me 262. Reportedly, there is no question that if the Germans had placed priority on the production of the Me 262, which entered development in 1939, the aerial war in Europe may have been theirs.[37]

By March 1945, two months before victory in Europe, Hitler's propaganda chief, Dr. Joseph Goebbels, wrote his thoughts about the final days of the air war in Europe:

> **Our Luftwaffe has gone totally to the dogs . . . The Americans now overfly German territory practically unresisted . . . [and] the damage done to our armaments potential is quite beyond repair . . . petrol available to the Luftwaffe has fallen from 193,000 tons to 8,800. What use is all this output of fighters when we have not even the petrol or crews to put them in action? The air war is still the great tale of woe . . . The situation becomes daily more intolerable and we have no means of defending ourselves against this catastrophe.[38]**

Field Marshals Albert Kesselring and Gerd von Rundstedt, considered two of the Third Reich's most astute and competent military leaders, were in agreement about Allied aerial power. In Kesselring's words, "Allied air power was the greatest single reason for the German defeat." And the chief of the Luftwaffe, Reichsmarshal Hermann Goering, just before his suicide in 1945, declared, "Without the United States Air Force the war would still be going on . . . [and] not on German soil."[39]

For the Allies, however, casualties had been high. During the 34th Bomb Group's 19,859 operational flying hours, approximately 3,574,600 air miles were flown by 30,679 airborne crewmen with a total of 3,197 sorties. The 34th Bomb Group delivered a total of 6,731 tons of bombs.[40]

During its 1,008 days in enemy action, the Eighth Air Force burned a billion gallons of gasoline, fired ninety-nine million rounds of machine gun ammunition, and expended 732,000 tons of bombs.[41]

All together, the Eighth Air Force lost 6,537 B-17s and B-24s. In addition, 3,337 fighters—our Little Friends—were destroyed.[42]

A total of 350,000 airmen served with the Eighth Air Force in England, and 26,000 were killed. Compared to the other branches of service, the Air Corps sustained the heaviest losses. More airmen in the Eighth lost their lives in World War II than in the entire Marine

Corps, whose enrollment included an excess of 250,000 men above and beyond those in the Eighth Air Force. In addition, another 21,000 men from the Eighth ended up in POW camps.[43]

Oddly, by the end of the war the casualties of the British and the Americans (who had entered the conflict much later) were almost exactly equal. The total losses from aerial combat in World War II reached 79,265 of those who served in the United States Army Air Force, and 79,281 who served with the RAF's Bomber Command, including Canadians, Australians, and New Zealanders.[44]

———————

When all is said and done, what remains beyond death and destruction, and the horrors of war, are strong friendships among those who served together in the war and survived. In the words of Gerald Astor, journalist, historian, and author of *The Mighty Eighth*:

> The kinship of those who served with the Eighth will not be replicated and indeed, it is not the same for them anymore. The intimacy of the bonds among those who lived together and faced death together comes only in the maw of war. But nevertheless, for many that time continues to burn brightly in their memories. And they can still draw satisfaction that they did end one terrible threat to our way of life.[45]

It is nearly impossible to find solace for those families who lost loved ones who served in the Eighth Air Force in England, the Ninth Air Force in France, the Twelfth and Fifteenth Air Force in Italy, the Royal Air Force, and the Luftwaffe. The lives of those we knew and those we did not know, will live in our hearts and minds forever. We can only honor their lives and the sacrifice they made for their country.

In a message to the 34th Bomb Group, General William E. Creer provided some comfort for those who served in the 34th and their families. This message, though, spoke to all men and women who have served their country in combat and reminds us of the common values and principles that guide our lives:

> As the former men of the 34th Bomb Group move on to peace-time achievements, their war accomplishments are likely to be

overshadowed. England in '44 and '45, as a part of their lives, will subside progressively into the past. However, it is hoped that experiences during this period will make each man wiser; and he will not forget how much war violates those principles by which we all live.[46]

May 8, 1945—VE Day   Victory in Europe became official at one minute after midnight in the early morning of May 8. The war in Europe, the devastation, the bombing, and the incineration was over.

The wartime pace at Mendlesham came to a grinding halt. B-17s rested at their hardstands; their engines quiet. The control tower was empty. I walked around the air base casually and enjoyed each step.

Celebrating VE Day at the 34th Bomb Group. (USAAF)

I'd stop and gaze up in the sky where I saw miles of tracks we had flown and paths we had crisscrossed many times before. I noticed things I had never seen before; the grass in the fields nearby was lovely with muted shades of green and yellow.

We felt rejuvenated without the constant tension, worry, fear, and anxiety. We were relaxed, peaceful, and at ease. We rode our bikes around the air base leisurely. We didn't have to check our watches every minute. No take-off and assembly. We didn't have that sinking feeling in our guts.

Colonel Creer would not allow anyone off the base for twenty-four hours. As odd as it may seem, most of us didn't want to go anyway. My crew attended one of the religious services held at the base chapel; the same service was repeated every hour all day. We sang the national anthem, and following the chaplain's sermon, scores of men's voices sang in chorus: "*Mine eyes have seen the glory of the coming of the Lord . . .*"

That night, guys were smoking cigars and Lucky Strikes, and drinking at the Officer's Club. The club was full and everyone was in the mood to celebrate. The joy was infectious and at times gave way to uncontrollable enthusiasm.

May 9, 1945   The Eighth Air Force requested that the 34th Bomb Group with other groups assist in the return of POWs from camps across Europe. Colonel Creer responded to this plea and asked for our support. After breakfast, we met with Colonel Creer at the control tower briefing room to get the details of this flight. We were to fly to Linz, Austria, and land at the Luftwaffe airfield just north of the city where a POW camp that held thousands of French prisoners had just been liberated. Every available plane of the 34th was scheduled to fly into Linz and return with at least twenty POWs each.

As the lead plane, we were the first to fly from the air base, and the 34th assembled in three squadrons behind us at five thousand feet. We flew over the Channel and headed east. I had asked Glen to monitor the radio for the group and he gave them our course. We climbed at the rate of three hundred feet a minute to nine thousand feet, and we estimated it would be a four-hour trip to Austria. As I looked below, it seemed so quiet and still as we passed over some of the bombed-out German cities where ruins now replaced once bustling urban centers.

Approaching the airfield in Linz, we flew in a regular flight pattern. We could see a landing strip that had been prepared for us. The strip bordered fields with scores of ruined fighters strewn about its perimeter. The makeshift runway had a long approach, and the army engineers had made room for all of us to park in the adjacent field. I landed, turned off the engines, took off the earphones and parachute harness, and lowered myself out the escape hatch. The other crews patiently waited in their planes for their orders. A jeep pulled up to greet us and a young army major stepped out and gave me a warm handshake.

"Welcome, Captain," he said. "It's great for you to respond so quickly to our request. We have thousands of prisoners in this camp, some of them have been here since the start of the war. As you can see, they're in terrible shape. They were just liberated yesterday and we've got a hell of a lot of work to do to straighten things out. I don't think there is a prisoner with identification. Most do not have dog tags and we will need to identify each one and determine the status of their health and the risk of disease. We need to de-louse each man as most are covered with bugs. Captain, tell me, what are your plans? When do you have to return to your base in England?"

"My orders call for us to be back before sunset, which would be about 7:00 P.M. British time. We should allow four and a half hours to return so we ought to leave by 2:30 P.M.." It was now 1:00 P.M.

"We're doing our level best and I hope we're going to have a number for you to take back but I'm not sure how many. When we put out the call to headquarters asking for planes to fly them out of here, we anticipated the process would be quite simple, but we were wrong. It's terribly involved, as I said, but we'll do our best. In the meantime, if any of your men would like to see Mauthausen, a few miles down the road, we would be glad to provide some trucks to take them down there. I don't encourage it, because it's a horrific sight. But if any wish to go, transportation is available." (Mauthausen was a holding camp for Jewish men before they were shipped to the gas chamber.)

I thanked the major and talked to the other crews, explaining the proximity of the German camp. I had to stay with *Miss Prudy* and I waited by her side in the event the major returned. Some of my guys left to see Mauthausen while the rest of the crews walked around the airfield looking at the vast array of discarded Luftwaffe war machines. I walked on the tarmac and picked up a few souvenirs: a German knife with a shield worn for formal occasions, an operating manual for an Me 262, and a piece of a wing of a German plane with a swastika on it. I sat in the cockpit of a Ju-88 for a brief moment. That was enough, and I left in a heartbeat.

As I walked around, I could not make eye contact with the prisoners behind the wire fence. Each held on to life, each patiently waited for his release with a hint of desperation and hope. I could not cope with the thought that I, a free man, was virtually helpless in aiding their release. I walked back to *Miss Prudy*. There was nothing I could do but wait.

By 2:30 P.M., the major drove up in his jeep. "I am terribly sorry," he said. "We cannot possibly give you any POWs to take back to Mendlesham. We are grossly unprepared for this job. We had no idea it would be so detailed and time consuming, and we only have a small staff to cope with this. Needless to say, there are language problems as well. Perhaps your group will be able to fly back in the next few days. Once we get the procedures underway, there will be a steady flow of prisoners ready to leave."

I promised to relay the message. We rounded up the men of the 34th and I encouraged all of the pilots to stay with me in reasonably close formation on the way back. I gave them our heading and estimated time of arrival, and we left empty-handed.

Once we were settled in flight, some of the crew told me about Mauthausen. There the atrocities of World War II were clearly visible. Many looked like skeletons, barely able to move, clinging to the wire fence, their fists in a tight grip. But they hung on to life with every ounce of will they had. Everything seemed as though it were still in operation, just on pause. An unforgiving odor of dying flesh permeated the camp; an odor my crew said they would never forget.

We had heard about German atrocities, but during the war we never knew the extent of what was happening. To this day, I still find it incomprehensible. The numbers were staggering. The concentration camps, I hope, will always serve as a reminder that man is capable of committing heinous crimes. We must never forget this dark time in history. Time may heal some of the wounds, but the atrocities must never be forgotten.

Two days later, the 34th returned to collect more than one thousand French prisoners, who were flown to Charles De Gaulle Airport in Paris. By this time, many bomb groups in the Eighth Air Force were returning POWs all over Europe, an enormous task repatriating tens of thousands of prisoners.

Eighth Air Force headquarters had one more request before we headed home. They asked that each pilot take ground personnel for a trip over western Germany and the Ruhr Valley to show how their tasks at the air base had contributed to our war effort. I took twenty non-commissioned officers on board. We flew up the Ruhr Valley and over Aachen, Duren, Frankfurt, Dusseldorf, and Cologne, where the beautiful cathedral miraculously still stood amidst the ruins.

During these days we waited for our departure to the States. Colonel Creer, determined that his men stay physically active and fit, encouraged our participation in team sports. The 34th challenged other bomb groups in all kinds of competitive games. We had a number of men skilled in track and field, including a national pole-vaulting champion, and we decided to enter the 34th in a meet at Felixstowe. I placed third in the 120-yard-high hurdles, walking off with a bronze medal which qualified me to compete with the Eighth Air Force Team.

The Eighth challenged the RAF to a track and field championship meet at London City Stadium. That's as far as I got. There were some fine performances, but as expected of war weary veterans, we did not break any records. We returned to our base with high hopes for our imminent departure to the States.

FAITH

Faith is not merely praying
Upon our knees at night:
Faith is not merely straying,
Through darkness into light:
Faith is not merely waiting
For Glory that may be—
Faith is the brave endeavor,
The splendid enterprise,
The strength to serve, whatever
Conditions may arise.

—S.E. Kiser[47]

13

Flying Home on a Wing and a Prayer

———◦•◦•◦———

W ord was out that we would be leaving soon to train in B-29s for service in the Pacific. Days before leaving, we learned that we would not be flying *Miss Prudy* home. She was to be flown to Allied Headquarters in Berlin, where she would be used to fly VIPs around Europe. Somehow that seemed fitting for a plane that I thought deserved recognition. Meanwhile, Glen and I were given orders to fly to an RAF field nearby to collect a B-17 that we would fly home.

When we saw our plane, we were downcast. It was painted black, unlike the sleek silver Flying Fortress we expected to see. This was a ghost ship. No one flew a black ship; that was bad luck. Clearly this plane had been used for covert operations and flown only at night. "Glen," I said, "we're never going to get anyone to fly this home with us, and I'm not sure I want to anyway!" When we returned to the base, we ran into Bill. "Come with us, we've got a terrible problem."

When Bill saw the plane, he said, "I'll tell you what we are going to do. I'll get some white paint and paint 'Ole Black Magic' on the side. That'll take the curse off it!"

Glen and I took *Ole Black* up a number of times, checking out each motor with great care, cutting engines and re-starting them, feathering all of them individually. Everything checked out beautifully, particularly the number four engine that had just been broken in with only thirty-four hours of flying time. We were ready for our flight home.

June 18, 1945 We received orders for our departure for the States. I was to fly back with my crew and ten non-commissioned officers. *Ole Black* would be carrying a plane of airmen and passengers with high expectations and hopes.

We shook hands with our friends in the 34th who were still at the base waiting for their departure. Before we gathered to leave, I needed time for one more goodbye. I walked over to *Miss Prudy,* climbed into my familiar cockpit, and sat down in a pilot's seat that was worn with memories. I placed my hand on the instrument panel and dropped my head forward, leaning gently on the steering wheel. I remembered so many times she had brought us back safely. I whis-

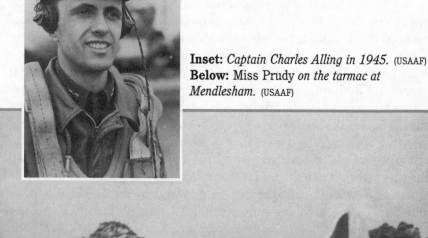

Inset: *Captain Charles Alling in 1945.* (USAAF)
Below: Miss Prudy *on the tarmac at Mendlesham.* (USAAF)

pered to her, keeping my voice low, though no one was near. "How did you do this? How did you bring us through?"

I marveled at her simplicity—I looked in the back of the plane where my crew had lived in this shell of steel. I marveled at her toughness and her durability. She was a mighty fortress, all right! I jumped out of the escape hatch for the final time. I walked on the tarmac along her side, stopped and looked up at *Miss Prudy*. She was tall and she was stately. I stood there for a moment, deep in thought, and looked down the runway that we had traveled together so many times. I turned to *Miss Prudy,* saluted her, and paused to take one last look that I will keep with me forever. Then I walked away with a pain that tugged at me inside, feeling that I had left a part of me behind. I never looked back; I couldn't do that. I could only look ahead to our return home.

It was time to leave. I climbed into *Ole Black*, battened down the hatches, and revved the engines. The hum of a B-17's engines, all so familiar, was soon going to be a sound of the past. I was actually feeling a little nostalgic. I looked out my window where I was accustomed to seeing our ground crew. For this final departure, though, there was no ground crew in sight, no thumbs up. Mendlesham was closing down and crews had been flying home. As my crew never did have their chance to buzz the base, I asked if we could just take *Ole Black* for one last circle over Mendlesham.

As we flew over the air base, I looked down at the control tower where I had often seen Colonel Creer standing on the open porch, keeping watch over his flock. Creer had left Mendlesham for the States a month earlier. I didn't imagine our paths would cross again. But I was comforted to know that if Creer were here today, he'd be watching us closely in his binoculars, and this time he wouldn't have to sweat it out. Every man who survived was his personal victory. I knew Creer had a lot of pride in the 34th Bomb Group. They were his men, and he had molded them into great pilots and crews.

We circled the Mendlesham airfield and made one final pass directly over the base before heading home. *Ole Black* dipped her wings gracefully and playfully in a final, simple farewell, packed with emotion and memory. I took one last look, said goodbye to Mendlesham, and carrying home a wealth of memories, westward we flew.

Our trip to the States was estimated to be a twenty-three-hour flight. We would cover thirty-four hundred miles from Mendlesham to the States; fifteen hundred of those miles were over the Atlantic. Our first stop was Prestwick, Scotland. After a brief rest in Prestwick, we left for Meek's Field at Reykjavik, Iceland, where the sun sets in the west and half an hour later, rises in the east. Shortly after take off, a weather front moved in from the east; but as expected, *Ole Black* sailed through without a hitch. We flew over the southeast tip of Iceland, and during our approach to Reykjavik, I couldn't help but notice the barren, windswept landscape and the small fishing boats that hugged the rugged coastline.

June 19, 1945   Ray, Bill, Glen, and I attended a briefing for our flight pattern and weather for the final leg of our trip. We were informed that due to the large number of planes flying from England to the States, the navy would maintain a bridge of ships in the northern Atlantic in case a plane had to ditch. This was unimaginable to me, and after all we had been through I could not understand why they were preparing for that possibility.

Our next stop was Goose Bay, Labrador—a fourteen-hundred-mile trip. Six hours later, we saw Greenland off our right wing and we anticipated making Goose Bay in four hours. Bill marveled at the blue pools of water at the tips of icebergs along the way. Greenland, the largest island in the world, seemed vast and desolate.

As part of my routine check, I monitored the designated high frequency radio station and checked all systems. Everything was fine. I settled into my seat. I felt calm, yet full of anticipation with the thought of returning home. I imagined walking up to the front door and greeting my family.

We were all in good spirits and I could hear Bill telling his jokes, followed by peels of laughter. I knew Ray was sitting beside Bill with a broad grin, and Willie too. I had never seen these guys so relaxed. We were each privately counting down the hours to our return home. Glen, Bill, Mort, Jack, and Willie each carried photographs of their wives, carefully tucked away in their coat pockets. I had Prudy's handwritten copy of the 23rd Psalm in my breast pocket. Our families knew we were flying back although they did not know our exact date of arrival. It was now at least ten days, if not more, since they had heard from us and I imagine they suspected we were en route.

Suddenly, a thunderous explosion shook *Ole Black*. I looked at all my instrument panels and I could feel the engines straining. I realized that number four engine, just broken in, had partially blown up and was virtually useless. Two piston rods had exploded, destroying the cylinders, and the cowling had blown off. One piece of the cowling had hit the exhaust of number three engine, which never functioned adequately from that moment on. Another part of the cowling hit the rudder, and the rudder pedals were vibrating so rapidly that I could not keep my feet on them. I had no rudder control, and could no longer make precise turns. I would now have to make slow turns using the ailerons.

I pressed the feathering button, keeping my thumb on it as hard as I could push. Slowly, thankfully, the prop of number four engine began slicing the air rather than acting as a brake. We started stalling and were losing altitude. To regain speed and altitude, I had to apply pressure on the remaining engines. I eased the throttles forward until the manifold pressure read thirty-eight inches—the pressure setting used for climbing only. I had no idea how long the remaining three engines could maintain that pressure.

I needed to redistribute weight toward the front of the plane. It was critically important to keep the nose down so that *Ole Black* would not stall out, so I asked all ground personnel to move as far forward as possible. They sat in the radio room, the bomb bay, the nose, and the pilot's compartment. Meanwhile, the crew went through the plane, tossing excess and heavy equipment. Guns and the auxiliary starter engine were the first to go. Even our luggage was thrown overboard with some of our mementos from the war, including our Eisenhower jackets with our decorations. The crew used a rifle butt to keep the escape hatch door open to throw out the gear. One piece of heavy equipment got entangled in the door hinge and nearly disengaged the door.

Eddie searched for the string of navy ships that we had expected to see, but he couldn't locate any. He tried to reach Goose Bay by radio, but the signal was too weak to continue a dialogue, although Eddie gathered that the base was closed due to inclement weather. I had two choices: either we try to reach Goose Bay or turn north to the Blue West Airstrip in Greenland, a hazardous strip, surrounded by mountains on three sides. Both were equidistant from our current location, but Labrador was on our route. I decided to try and reach Labrador.

Minutes later, we spotted a B-24 Liberator flying at the same altitude just a few miles away. I called on the radio frequency, "B-24, B-24. Do you see a B-17, color black, flying off your left wing?"

"Roger, we see you B-17. Looks like you're about to stall out."

"Our number four engine is gone and we're now just above stalling speed. Who are you B-24?"

The pilot replied, "This is Captain Armentrout, B-17. If you're heading to Goose Bay, why don't we fly along with you as long as we can. We'll keep circling around you as we cannot travel so slowly. If anything happens, the least we can do is give a radio fix to other planes and ships. I'll do whatever I can, B-17. By the way, B-17, who are you?"

"Captain Alling," I replied. "Thanks for keeping an eye on us."

We were four hundred miles from the Goose Bay airfield and flying against headwinds at a ground speed of only 108 miles per hour. We were three and a half hours from landing. I checked and re-checked the engines for power settings, overheating, and oil pressure. Willie never took his eyes off them. The Wright Cyclone engines were not designed to withstand such pressure and now they would have to stay with us far beyond their specification. We were also running the risk of damaging the remaining engines in the process, and I knew that we would be burning more fuel on three engines than four.

Once more, Eddie made it through to the radio station at Goose Bay, and this time the connection was clear. They suggested we go on to Gander, Newfoundland, because of poor visibility. Eddie relayed the news to me. "Eddie," I said, "we need to inform Goose Bay to get out all their equipment. We're coming in, and we have no choice."

Eddie called in again, "This is an emergency, Goose Bay. We only have three engines running. We're coming in."

"Okay B-17. Stay in touch. We wish you the best of luck," Goose Bay replied.

The minutes seemed interminable. Our passengers were having a tough time and some, who had rarely flown, were nearly frantic. Glen reported in: "Bill's having trouble with a passenger who is desperate and trying to escape through the hatch. It looks like Bill's trying to calm him down."

"Pilot to bombardier. Pilot to bombardier," I called. No answer.

"Pilot to bombardier," I called again, and still no answer. Time seemed to stand still with impending chaos on board.

"Chuck," Bill finally called in. "I've got him pinned down. We're under control. Don't worry."

Ray was soon able to get weak signals from the Cape Harrison radio at the closest point of land in Labrador. By averaging several bearings, he got an acceptable one that provided him with a direct course over the water. The sun was in a perfect position for him to get a Line of Position reading that cut the course line at about ninety degrees. This provided him with a fairly accurate fix and accurate ground speed which was about one hundred knots most of the time. Bill assisted Ray in taking readings based on their interpretation of the drift from the white caps.

As we flew along, the silence was frightening. The only noise in the plane was the sound of the engines and the vibration of the rudder pedals. There wasn't anything anyone could do but hope and pray. The passengers sat on the floor in the cockpit. No one looked up. No one moved. They stared at the floor, their thoughts miles away. Some held good luck charms in their fingers, some whispering an occasional Hail Mary. Others clasped photos of loved ones in their hands.

I looked down at the icebergs; this was an impossible place to try to land or ditch a plane. I wondered about death. What would it be like? Was it painful? Was this the way it was meant to end? Was our time up? My heart was pounding.

I looked at the engine instruments, most of which were on the co-pilot's side. The oil pressure on engine one and two were fine, but number three engine was low, although slightly above the red mark. While Glen was in charge of the intercom, I monitored the high frequency station which all pilots checked as closely as they could. It was alarmingly still until Armentrout checked in, "Alling," he called, "I didn't get permission to land at Goose Bay either, but I told them I had to because I was flying as your escort. I can see it's getting dark ahead, and if the weather is bad, I may not be able to stay with you all the way, but I'll do what I can."

"Thanks Captain. When it's time, you'll have to keep going and I understand," I replied.

"OK, we have just under two hours to go," I explained to the passengers and crew. "We're doing as well as we can. Have faith. I believe we'll get there." I was trying to convince my crew and passengers of something that I was privately trying to believe myself.

It was impossible to fly this plane without adjustments and I continually worked the throttles back to reduce the manifold pressure. It had been an hour since we had lost engine four. Now we were carrying a lighter load after we had burned up several hundred gallons of gas and thrown out most of our heavy gear, so I was able to bring down the manifold pressure.

Looking down at the ocean, I noticed that the icebergs were beginning to thin out. That was a good sign. Ray reminded me that the airfield was a twenty-five minute flight from the coast. Once over land, we could bail out if we had to, although that would still be horrendous and rescuers would have a tough time finding us. Even still, I knew it was virtually impossible to ditch safely. We could not find a clear path between the icebergs, and even if we could, we would not survive in the ice cold water.

My mind raced. I looked over at Glen and then at Willie seated on the jump seat between us. Neither took their eyes off the instruments. I looked at the engines, and somehow they were still running smoothly. If one of the three engines cut out, *Ole Black* would stall against those headwinds and drop from the sky.

We flew into puffs of cumulus, and Armentrout's plane was lost for several seconds in the clouds. I knew we couldn't keep him with us much longer and I called him on the radio. "I think you better go on ahead. You're probably getting low on fuel."

"I was just going to call you. I think that makes sense. Good luck," he said, "I know I'll see you at the base. I'll be there waiting for you."

I hoped that he was right. We were in the clouds flying on instruments. I knew that I would have to make a landing on our first attempt, regardless of the weather and poor visibility. We were now an hour and a half from the airfield. Our number three engine had become more erratic and I could feel the strain of numbers one and two. I could not apply any more manifold pressure or the engines would blow up.

Time was now interminable. Finally Ray called in, "By my calculations, we should be going over Indian Harbor, the closest point of land, in five minutes. We'll follow the Hamilton Inlet west until we come to Lake Melville and then we'll see the airfield."

"Alright, Ray. Great job! Just let me know when we have ten minutes to go," I said, feeling slightly relieved.

Fifteen minutes from the air strip, we began a slow descent of three hundred feet per minute. If our calculations were correct, that would put us on the runway and also give us enough altitude in case we had to parachute and suddenly ditch the plane.

"Glen, how much gas do we have?" I asked, not really wanting to know the answer.

"I didn't want to tell you," he replied, "I've been trying to keep the tanks evenly distributed in each wing, and they register empty."

I felt sick, but somehow *Ole Black* kept flying. The cloud cover remained thick, and still there was no sign of life below, no sign of land.

Ray called in: "ETA is ten minutes, Chuck."

"Okay guys. We're getting close," I said, hoping everyone would feel encouraged.

I started our descent, knowing full well we were now over a deep lake at the eastern approach to the landing strip, and that we would continue to fly over water until we touched down. I knew Bill and Ray were searching for land, searching for a small air strip in a vast stretch of wilderness. We were now five minutes from the Goose Bay airfield and there was no sign of land. I wanted to descend faster to find a break in the clouds. "Ray," I called, "I'm hitting the deck. I'm going down to 100 feet."

"Go for it!" he called back with confidence.

We couldn't fly much lower. We had no choice but to be dead on target. There was no room for a mistake or minor error in our calculation. A slight variance from our course would put us belly up on the river or we would crash in the forest that bordered the water's edge. We descended slowly and cautiously, and with each second I wondered whether we were approaching the airfield or the water. I waited and waited, listening to the strain of the engines and the intense vibration of the rudder. And then, to our complete disbelief, we saw land.

"There it is! There it is!" Glen shouted. In a momentary break in the clouds, we saw the airstrip about five miles ahead. We were in a perfect line with the strip. Ray had done it again! He was always on target and never let us down. Even under extreme duress, Ray had charted a brilliant course!

"Ray, you did it! You did it!" I called into the intercom. I was not amazed, because I believed in Ray; I just felt an overwhelming sense of gratitude to him and *Ole Black*. The crew and passengers took a deep breath and quietly sighed their relief. We still had a way to go, but now I believed that we would make it after all.

I waited a minute and then called in, "Flaps one third," and I paused for a few seconds. "Slowly . . ." I held my breath, wondering if the flaps had been damaged by metal from the engine cowling when it blew off. I knew that if a piece of number four engine had hit the rudder, other pieces could have hit and damaged the flaps on the right wing, potentially leaving them unusable as well. Flaps were critical in the landing process; they served as a lift to compensate for the reduced engine power and cutting the airspeed for a safe landing. If the flaps were to lower on one side only, the drag created on that side could flip the plane over. But quite miraculously, the flaps moved in unison on both wings, and I could feel the plane lift just as the airspeed slightly reduced, just as I had hoped.

"Flaps down! Wheels down!" I called to Glen, and I waited for a few terrifying moments filled with anxiety.

"Full flaps! Wheels down!" Glen responded, his voice sounding assured and confident. That was music to my ears. *Ole Black* was a great workhorse and she was plowing steadily through the very last few minutes of this harrowing journey.

Focusing on a spot three hundred feet short of the runway, I aimed there for touchdown. Most pilots go beyond the start of the runway, if for no other reason than apprehension. I only had one chance to make it; we could never take a second pass.

We were now a mile away, still flying over the dark lake, and number three engine started to sputter. At last, we approached the edge of the shore. I pulled back the engine throttles and we continued our gradual descent. The end of the runway was still forty or fifty feet away. I couldn't haul back anymore. We were slowing down, but even still, *Ole Black* was eating up runway. Then we heard the screech of the tires on the tarmac. We greased it—rubber to tar! I waited for the tail wheel to touch. It touched. I pressed on the brakes. We were going to stop in time with even a little room to spare. Then we came to a grinding halt just as number three engine sputtered out.

Absurdly, out of habit, I called to Glen, "Taxi instructions."

"Chuck, cut the engines," Glen replied. "We're not taxiing—we can't. We don't have a drop of gas left. The tower says bail out and leave the plane at the end of the runway." I looked over to acknowledge his reply. Glen's face was pale and he seemed dazed.

As the props wheezed and stopped, nineteen guys jumped out of the exits and kissed the ground. Glen was the last of my crew to make his way toward the escape hatch. Speechless, we couldn't say anything, nor did we need to. I was full of wonder that we had made it safely, and I know Glen felt the same way. Moments later, Glen stood up, a bit shaky, and gently lowered himself through the escape hatch while I stayed seated, alone.

I patted the instrument panel and thanked *Ole Black* for bringing us here, knowing full well we should never have made it. *Ole Black*, after all our misgivings, was a stalwart plane that had carried nineteen grateful men back to a place not far from where we had left ten months before.

I must have sat there by myself for several minutes. Exhausted and depleted, I didn't have an ounce of strength left. I stripped off my parachute harness and placed my earphones on the instrument panel. I looked up to the sky and thanked God for being with us. I let my head fall forward, sinking into my cupped hands, and my eyes filled with tears.

Moments later, I'm not sure exactly how long, I looked back up into the deep, boundless sky, toward a place where I imagined heaven must be, a place where I believed Prudy rested peacefully. I had a sudden, unmistakable feeling of clarity and understanding, and I must have smiled, for everything made sense to me. "Prudy," I whispered, "you are an angel. You stayed with me the whole time. You were *always* there with me like an angel on my wings." I stood up from my seat, walked toward the escape hatch, eased myself through, dropping down to the tarmac and onto my knees, and unashamedly kissed the ground.

The Miracle of Memory

When I was young and strong
Things were different then.
I thought I'd live forever
That the good times would never end.

But now I see things differently,
I look back, not just ahead
Recalling as if it was yesterday
Things I've done and said.

I find things neatly stored away
In the recesses of my mind,
And each time I search I'm overwhelmed
By the treasures that I find!

There are all my yesterdays
Laid neatly in a row,
Filled to the brim with all those things
I put there long ago.

This treasure house of memories
Is held exclusively for me.
No one else can use them
I have the only key.

Matching half-remembered stories
With half-remembered faces,
I begin to place them once again
In those half-forgotten places.

I relive those precious moments
Laid aside so long before
But now brought back, through the miracle of memory,
To enrich my life once more!

—William L. Wright
Group Lead Bombardier, *Miss Prudy*
Eighth Air Force, England   1944–1945

14

Afterword

——◆◆——

The last leg of our journey was just around the corner. When we arrived, Captain Armentrout was waiting for us at the base lodge as promised. I walked up to this tall, commanding man, "You must be Captain Armentrout," I said.

"And you must be Captain Alling!" he responded with a sense of relief, and we shook hands.

"I can't thank you enough for staying with us!" We spoke for a while and he told me he was returning to the States the next morning.

"Captain Alling," he said, "I hope to see you back in the States." I hoped so, too.

That night I slept for seventeen hours, rising in time for a complete American breakfast. In late morning, the base commander approached me. "Captain Alling, we have an engine for you that will be ready to go tomorrow, but we'll have to fly an engine cowling in from the States. Unfortunately, you're here until it arrives. We'll give you a couple of jeeps so you can explore and go fishing. There are trout streams nearby. The Officer's Club is stocked with good novels and cards. There are pool tables and they'll run some movies off for you, too. All phones are off limits except for emergencies. When you get to the States, you'll be able to make calls courtesy of Uncle Sam." But that didn't matter; we were just happy to be on the last leg of our journey. Besides, none of us had talked on the phone for months.

The engine cowling arrived the next day and Glen, Willie, and I took *Ole Black* for a test run. We worked the new engine as hard as we dared, feathered the props, and cut the power off and on. All systems were go. I looked at my companions. "What do you say we go?" I asked. "There's no sense waiting!" I said. We all agreed it was time to head home, and so I asked the base commander for clearance for departure.

"Sure," he replied, "I'll take care of it right away." We gathered our crew and passengers, each eager to take the last flight.

June 23, 1945 We left for our final destination, Bradley Field, in Windsor Locks, Connecticut—a five-and-a-half-hour flight from Goose Bay. We flew south through Quebec Province, over Montreal and into Vermont. As we crossed the border, there was a spontaneous cheer. It was easy from there on.

After we landed at Bradley Field, we were met by jeeps and off we went to the dining hall for a buffet dinner of filet mignon, Maine lobsters, corn on the cob, and fifteen varieties of thick, creamy ice-cream and chocolate syrup. After dinner, we made calls home. I called Montclair. "I'm in the States. I'm here. I'm coming home!" I couldn't believe what I was saying. "Tomorrow, I'll take the train to New York and then Montclair. I'll grab a taxi home, sometime in the afternoon!"

It was time for each one of us to return to our towns across the country. I left for Montclair, New Jersey; Glen Banks headed for Mingo Junction, Ohio; Ray Baskin returned to Mason, Tennessee; Bill Wright raced back to his wife, Nell, in New Smyrna Beach, Florida; Willie Green took the most direct route home to his wife in Tuscumb, Alabama; Mort Narva took the train back to Newark, New Jersey; Eddie Edwards returned to Pitcairn, Pennsylvania; Jack Brame rejoined his wife in Topeka, Kansas; and Chuck Williams flew across the country to be with his wife and son in Berkeley, California. We were granted a thirty-day leave, and at the end of our leave, we had orders to meet in Sioux Falls, South Dakota, a staging center for deployment and reassignment. We were anxious to get home, and knowing we'd see each other soon, we didn't feel the need to say goodbye.

I had almost completed the final leg of my journey from Mendlesham to Montclair, and as I approached my home, the eight-minute ride up the hill from the Montclair railroad station seemed unreal. I couldn't believe I was nearly there. The taxi driver, a young guy my age, was eager to talk about the war. He noticed the ribbons and decorations sewn on my jacket, and couldn't control himself any longer, "Were you a pilot overseas?" And so we talked. "What's your name?" he asked. I told him, and he thought for a moment. "Is your father, Charles?"

"Yes," I responded with pride.

"Is he head of the Draft Board in town?"

"Yes," I answered with pride.

"Do you know your father gave me a deferment from serving in the army? He knew I had a family of nine to support, but he let his own son go to war."

"Makes sense to me," I said. "He's quite a guy and you're about to meet him."

The taxi pulled up at the curb. My parents and sisters, Joan and Betty, cousins, neighbors, and Peter, my collie, were waiting near the edge of the sidewalk, eagerly anticipating my taxi to turn the corner. After we rounded the bend, I stepped out of the cab into the warm embrace of my family that lasted longer than I can recall. Peter jumped up and looked at me with his imploring eyes, barked and launched into his victory cry. This time, he sensed I was home for good.

I walked across the porch and into my house where everything looked the same—the furniture, the upholstery was the same, just a bit faded. It seemed that nothing had changed; it was almost as if time had stopped in Montclair. But it was different for me. If I had taken snapshots of my life over the past ten months, I'd have seen a face that had changed with increments of time, now a bit older, a bit wiser.

———————— ⋅•◆•⋅ ————————

I don't know what happened to my crew during our leave. My father and I went camping near Mt. Katahdin, Maine, for ten days, and we did not see another person with the exception of our guide. I listened to the rustle of the wind in the pine trees and I was lulled by the sounds of the water lapping on the banks of the Penobscot River. We took long walks, and we fished in the river. We were worlds apart from where I had been, and at peace in this solitude.

I don't remember telling my father much about the war, but I do recall the pleasure of being with him. Our time together was a testimony to our relationship, and to much of what I had learned about life. He had always been instrumental in guiding me and teaching me about friendships and values—values that I would draw upon like a lifelong supply from a well. Our friendship was different than the friendships and bonds I formed with my crew, but each friendship was significant in its own way.

During those peaceful nights in Maine, I'd look up at the stars just as I had done in Mendlesham when the war in Europe came to an end. In Mendlesham, I could map the paths I had traveled from star to star. But here, the paths between the stars were not worn, the sky above was clear and not traveled. I knew it wouldn't be long before I would map a new course in life in uncharted territory.

At the end of my leave, I left for Sioux Falls, South Dakota. This air base was expansive, and I spent hours trying to track down each one of my crew among thousands of airmen who had just returned from combat in Europe. We were all scattered around the base, waiting for our next assignments. Days after my arrival in Sioux Falls, I was transferred to Deming, New Mexico, where lead pilots were trained as operations officers. While I was able to track down each one of my crew in Sioux Falls, I sadly never did get a chance to say a final goodbye because of my sudden and unexpected departure.

Upon arriving in Deming, I walked into the officer's barracks and went straight to my room to drop off my bag. I turned around to introduce myself to my roommate. To my astonishment, it was Captain Armentrout, who had escorted us to the Goose Bay airfield.

"Alling!" he smiled and we shook hands again, "My God, Alling, great to see you! Did they give you clearance to land this time?"

While I was in Deming, I had a lot of time to think about my crew and I wondered where their next assignments would take them. My abrupt departure from Sioux Falls gave me a pained feeling of emptiness and loss that I had to put behind me as I moved ahead with my next assignment, and they with theirs.

I missed their presence, the close friendships, their constant companionship and humor, and their complete, knowing, and sometimes unspoken understanding. I had to believe that nothing could ever take that away—and nothing ever did.

Fall, 1945 The war was over with the horrific and finite bomb-ings in Japan. That quickly became the end of my life as a pilot—I never did fly a B-17 again, nor did I want to.

In keeping with family tradition, I entered Yale University, trans-ferring from Wesleyan, and began my junior year in September 1945. My roommate was Dick Gates, brother of Gordy Gates, my dear friend who died in the Pacific. Dick had just finished his tour of duty as a P-51 Mustang pilot with the 352nd Fighter Group in the Eighth Air Force stationed in Bodney, England.

One fall weekend, I was on my way home from Yale. I took the train from New Haven, and was seated next to a high school class-mate, Johnny Carter. Johnny told me that he had also been a B-17 pilot in the Eighth Air Force. His bomber was shot down by the Luftwaffe and he had spent two years in a POW camp near Dresden, Germany. I shuddered at the thought of being trapped in a POW camp near Dresden during the air raids on the city. I listened intent-ly and he focused on the Eighth Air Force raid of March 2. Johnny then said, "If I ever find the American B-17 pilot who led the Eighth Air Force that day, I'm going to kill him!"

I looked at him, not knowing what to say, or if I should say any-thing at all. I decided it was better to let the subject fade away.

Months later, I walked up to Johnny at a Christmas party. We were talking and I had to ask him, "Do you still feel the same way about that American pilot who led the March 2nd raid over Dresden?"

"No, I don't," he said, "but someday, I'd really like to know who that guy was."

"Johnny," I said, "You're looking at him."

"You SOB, Alling!" And then he smiled in an understanding way as if he felt resolved about everything. "Hey, I guess we're both damn lucky to be alive, aren't we? But, God damn it, Alling!"

I knew there were many guys like Johnny Carter and me, each with different war experiences who were more than fortunate to return home. And I also knew I was fortunate to return with friends who had flown with me side by side.

When I first joined my crew, we were a bunch of guys with enough will to meet the test of endurance. We flew those mighty planes with a clear and disciplined mind. We made it through the war with luck on our side and faith in our hearts. Those months of training fortified each one of us: our will, our hope and faith, so that nothing could unravel our spirit and sheer determination.

Looking back, my war experience had a lot to do with who I was, my values and the way I would lead my life. Once I had returned to my country, my family, and friends, I picked up from where I left off, feeling a little weary, but much stronger from it all.

In 1985, I decided to retrace my steps overseas and I traveled back to the Mendlesham air base with eighty-three airmen of the 34th Bomb Group. Our gathering marked the fortieth anniversary of VE Day. We met at Heathrow Airport whereupon we traveled to Ipswich for dinner and a night's stay at the Post House. Everyone was anxious to tell his stories about the 34th. During this time, I was aware that William Creer was in this group of returning visitors. No longer a colonel, Creer was a major general. I had such deep respect for him, I couldn't muster the courage to introduce myself.

The next morning, we visited Mendlesham. The air base looked worn with time. The runways were covered with weeds, the Nissen huts seemed to sag and list to one side, their metal roofs corroded and rusted. The control tower was empty, forgotten, and deserted.

General Creer led a ceremony for the 34th Bomb Group at the Mendlesham base, and laid a wreath on a memorial. The inscription on the bronze plaque placed at the westerly end of the main runway reads:

To the American airmen of the 34th Bomb Group (H) who in valor gave their lives to the victory that made real the challenge for world peace and unity.[48]

Beautiful flowers lay at the base of the memorial. We were told that the townspeople brought freshly cut flowers to the memorial every day as they have done for the past forty years.

Later, we had lunch at the King's Head Pub in Mendlesham, and there I decided to introduce myself to Creer as I had not seen him in forty years. Even though there were many in the group still waiting their chance to talk with him, a path finally cleared. I summoned my courage, and made my way over to him. I reached out my hand, "General Creer, I am Chuck Alling, one of your pilots."

He put his arms around me, "Alling, you son of a gun! I've been wondering when the heck you were going to get the nerve to come over here! Alling, you were one of my favorite pilots!" And there we stood together and talked about the war and the 34th Bomb Group. Just as I would expect, he never missed a beat, recalling life at Mendlesham, some of the more harrowing missions, and the mercy mission we flew together over Rotterdam. Those few minutes brought a closure to my life at the air base, and I was fortunate to have the opportunity to recognize a distinguished man whom I admired and respected as our leader.

The final day of our reunion, we were bussed to the American Cemetery at Madingly near Cambridge, where thousands of Eighth Air Force airmen have been laid to rest. We walked through the cemetery just minutes before a service to commemorate the fortieth anniversary of Victory Europe.

We stood at the bottom of this hill and looked up at the white crosses each inscribed with a name, serial number, and unit number of an airman. Slowly, I made my way up the hill through rows of white crosses. Each step weighed heavily on my mind, and each step was profound as I passed by gravesites of many who flew in the Eighth Air Force, a few I may have known.

At the top of the hill, there was a wall of Italian marble that listed the name of each man buried in the cemetery. A reflecting pool stood at the base of the wall where the inscription of names shimmered in the sunlit water. Facing the wall, on the right side, there was a marble platform bordered by honor guards with the Union Jack and the Stars and Stripes waving in the soft breeze. We sat down on folding chairs on the platform along with dignitaries, an RAF band, Air Force band, and choir of one hundred women dressed in white. Hundreds of townspeople stood nearby for the service.

The service lasted exactly one hour with speeches and hymns. The RAF band played "God Save The Queen" and the Air Force band followed with "The Star Spangled Banner." The service came to a close with a nineteen-gun musket volley fired by a platoon of riflemen, and taps as the lonely, haunting sound of the trumpet echoed through the hills and valleys. And then, precisely an hour from the start of the service, a squadron of British jets approached the cemetery and flew directly over us, in tight formation, leaving a definite and formidable path in the sky, sending shudders up my spine. That moment brought tears to my eyes, and that's when I knew I had seen life in all its glory.

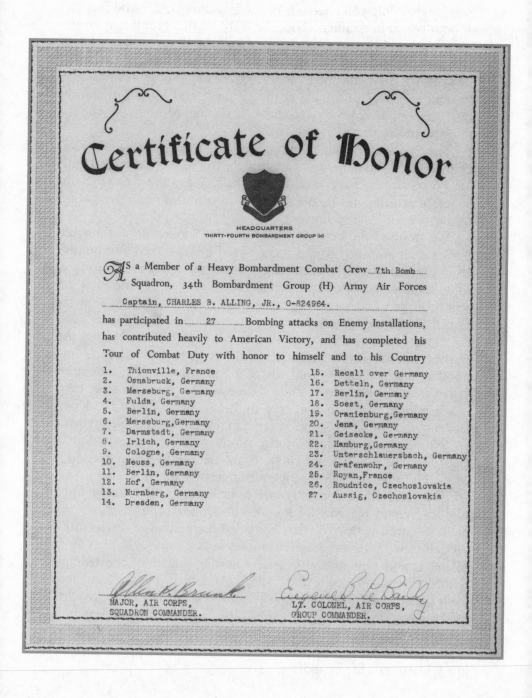

Certificate of Honor

HEADQUARTERS
THIRTY-FOURTH BOMBARDMENT GROUP (H)

As a Member of a Heavy Bombardment Combat Crew 7th Bomb Squadron, 34th Bombardment Group (H) Army Air Forces Captain, CHARLES B. ALLING, JR., O-824964.

has participated in 27 Bombing attacks on Enemy Installations, has contributed heavily to American Victory, and has completed his Tour of Combat Duty with honor to himself and to his Country

1. Thionville, France
2. Osnabruck, Germany
3. Merseburg, Germany
4. Fulda, Germany
5. Berlin, Germany
6. Merseburg, Germany
7. Darmstadt, Germany
8. Irlich, Germany
9. Cologne, Germany
10. Neuss, Germany
11. Berlin, Germany
12. Hof, Germany
13. Nurnberg, Germany
14. Dresden, Germany
15. Recall over Germany
16. Detteln, Germany
17. Berlin, Germany
18. Soest, Germany
19. Oranienburg, Germany
20. Jena, Germany
21. Geisecke, Germany
22. Hamburg, Germany
23. Unterschlauersbach, Germany
24. Grafenwohr, Germany
25. Royan, France
26. Roudnice, Czechoslovakia
27. Aussig, Czechoslovakia

MAJOR, AIR CORPS,
SQUADRON COMMANDER.

LT. COLONEL, AIR CORPS,
GROUP COMMANDER.

Endnotes

1. *On War Against Japan: Franklin D. Roosevelt's "Day of Infamy" Address of 1941.* Washington, DC: National Archives and Records Administration, 1988.
2. *1,000 Quotable Poems: An Anthology of Modern Verse.* Compiled by Thomas Curtis Clark and Esther A. Gillespie. New York: Gramercy Books, 2000.
3. *1,000 Quotable Poems: An Anthology of Modern Verse.* New York: Gramercy Books, 2000.
4. Kaplan, Philip and Smith, Rex Alan, *One Last Look.* New York: Abbeville Press, 1983.
5. Hatch, Gardener, *Thirty-Fourth Bombardment Group (H)1941-1945.* Paducah, KY: Turner Publishing Company, 1988.
6. "Thirteen Hundred Heavies Pound Metz." *Stars and Stripes*, 1944.
7. Hatch, Gardener, *Thirty-Fourth Bombardment Group (H)1941-1945.* Paducah, KY: Turner Publishing Company, 1988.
8. *1,000 Quotable Poems: An Anthology of Modern Verse.* New York: Gramercy Books, 2000.
9. *The Taste of Courage: The War, 1939-1945.*, ed. by Desmond Flower and James Reeves. New York: Harper & Brothers Publishers, 1960.
10. Graham, Frederick, *The New York Times.* New York: April 20, 1945.
11. Hatch, Gardener, *Thirty-Fourth Bombardment Group (H)1941-1945.* Paducah, KY: Turner Publishing Company, 1988.
12. *1,000 Quotable Poems: An Anthology of Modern Verse.* New York: Gramercy Books, 2000.
13. Hatch, Gardener, *Thirty-Fourth Bombardment Group (H)1941-1945.* Paducah, KY: Turner Publishing Company, 1988.
14. *1,000 Quotable Poems: An Anthology of Modern Verse.* New York: Gramercy Books, 2000.
15. Kaplan, Philip and Smith, Rex Alan, *One Last Look.* New York: Abbeville Press, 1983.

16. Hatch, Gardener, *Thirty-Fourth Bombardment Group (H) 1941-1945.* Paducah, KY: Turner Publishing Company,1988.
17. Hatch, Gardener, *Thirty-Fourth Bombardment Group (H) 1941-1945.* Paducah, KY: Turner Publishing Company,1988.
18. Granberg, Herbe, *Aftonbladet,* Stockholm, 1945.
19. Hatch, Gardener, *Thirty-Fourth Bombardment Group (H) 1941-1945.* Paducah, KY: Turner Publishing Company,1988.
20. Hatch, Gardener, *Thirty-Fourth Bombardment Group (H) 1941-1945.* Paducah, KY: Turner Publishing Company,1988.
21. Hatch, Gardener, *Thirty-Fourth Bombardment Group (H) 1941-1945.* Paducah, KY: Turner Publishing Company,1988.
22. Archives Section Library. Maxwell Air Force Base, Montgomery, AL.
23. Combat Chronology 1941-1945. U.S. Army Air Forces in World War II.
24. Boyne, Walter J., *Clash of Wings: World War II In The Air.* New York: Touchstone, 1994.
25. Huchthausen, Peter, "Collateral Damage." *The York County Coast Star,* 7 July 1999.
26. *1,000 Quotable Poems: An Anthology of Modern Verse.* New York: Gramercy Books, 2000.
27. Middleton, Drew, *The New York Times,* 22 June 1945.
28. *1,000 Quotable Poems: An Anthology of Modern Verse.* New York: Gramercy Books, 2000.
29. Crosby, Harry H.: *A Wing And A Prayer: The "Bloody 100th" Bomb Group Of The U.S. Eighth Air Force In Action Over Europe In World War II.* New York: HarperCollins Publishers, 1993.
30. *1,000 Quotable Poems: An Anthology of Modern Verse.* New York: Gramercy Books, 2000.
31. Maass, Walter B., *The Netherlands At War: 1940-1945.* London, New York, Toronto: Abelard-Schuman,1970.
32. Smith, Edwin S., *The History of the Army Air Forces 34th BOM-BARDMENT Group (H).* San Angelo, TX: Newsfoto Publishing Co., 1947.
33. Smith, Edwin S., *The History of the Army Air Forces 34th BOM-BARDMENT Group (H).* San Angelo, TX: Newsfoto Publishing Co., 1947.
34. *1,000 Quotable Poems: An Anthology of Modern Verse.* New York: Gramercy Books, 2000.
35. *Germany Surrenders 1945.* Washington, DC: National Archives and Records Administration, 1989.
36. *Germany Surrenders 1945.* Washington, DC: National Archives and Records Administration, 1989.
37. Boyne, Walter J., *Clash of Wings.* New York: Touchstone, 1994.

38. Kaplan, Philip and Smith, Rex Alan, *One Last Look*. New York: Abbeville Press, 1983.
39. Kaplan, Philip and Smith, Rex Alan, *One Last Look*. New York: Abbeville Press, 1983.
40. Hatch, Gardener, *Thirty-Fourth Bombardment Group (H) 1941-1945*. Paducah, KY: Turner Publishing Company, 1988.
41. Kaplan, Philip and Smith, Rex Alan, *One Last Look*. New York: Abbeville Press, 1983.
42. Astor, Gerald, *The Mighty Eighth: The Air War in Europe as Told by the Men Who Fought It*. New York: Dell Publishing, 1997.
43. Astor, Gerald, *The Mighty Eighth*. New York: Dell Publishing, 1997.
44. Clodfelter, Micheal. *Warfare And Armed Conflicts. A Statistical Reference to Casualty and Other Figures, 1681-1991, Vol. II*. Jefferson, North Carolina and London: McFarland & Company, 1992.
45. Astor, Gerald, *The Mighty Eighth*. New York: Dell Publishing, 1997.
46. Smith, Edwin S., *The History of the Army Air Forces 34th BOMBARDMENT Group (H)*. San Angelo, TX: Newsfoto Publishing Co., 1947.
47. *1,000 Quotable Poems: An Anthology of Modern Verse*. New York: Gramercy Books, 2000.
48. Smith, Edwin S., *The History of the Army Air Forces 34th BOMBARDMENT Group (H)*. San Angelo, TX: Newsfoto Publishing Co., 1947.

Index